DAWN
TO
DUSK

The 1996 Methodist Companion

Dawn to Dusk
© Methodist Publishing House, 1995

Illustrations © Steven Hall

ISBN 1 85852 046 0

CONTENTS

FOREWORD

The best of books are like good friends, ever ready to share with us from the riches of their experience. *Dawn to Dusk* will prove to be just such a good friend.

You will find in its pages the voices of men and women of our day, who will share with you their responses to living with the strenuous demands and painful concerns of the late twentieth century. Sometimes the mood is one of thankfulness and joy, often there is a quiet serenity and hopefulness, but sometimes they voice doubts and fears for themselves and for those whom they love, as well as revealing both compassion and indignation at the sufferings of others.

They are surrounded by a cloud of witnesses, voices from the distant past as well as from our own century, who in letters and diaries, essays and sermons, novels and poetry, reflected on their experiences in the light of what they believed. Their life's setting may be as different from our own as the medieval monastery of Thomas à Kempis. Their experiences may be as agonising as the tortured existence of William Cowper and John Clare. They may be important historical figures like the Wesleys or Julian of Norwich. Yet so very often they are unexpectedly one with us in their own questioning. *Their* love helps us to renew *our* compassion and forbearance. *Their* confessed moments of stress and doubt make them fellow pilgrims with *us*, and we hear them with greater respect because we know that spiritually they have sat where we now sit.

DAWN TO DUSK

You can pick up this new friend in a moment of rest from an all too busy life, or browse comfortably in retirement. You can open it at random and discover a voice that sounds strangely like your own. You can put down the book and meditate upon a truth which you knew but never understood so clearly as now. You can come fresh to its pages or read and re-read pages which have already gripped you and still find new understanding of our human lot, and perhaps experience renewed faith, hope and love.

Place the book just where you can reach it without rising from your easy chair! Or better still, leave it on your coffee table where one of your family or a visitor may pick it up and find light for their everyday life or a greater depth to their faith. This is a book you will want to share!

Frank Collier

2

PRAISE
&
THANKSGIVING

It is a praiseworthy thing to be perfectly
acquainted with God, that is, to recognise
that he is incomprehensible; and recognising him
thus, to love him, and loving him to rejoice in him;
and rejoicing, to rest in him;
and in quiet to arrive at
eternal rest.

Richard Rolle,
The Fire of Love

This day, by God's mercy, I am twenty nine years of age, and in very good health and like to live and get an estate; and if I have a heart to be contented, I think I may reckon myself as happy a man as any is in the world – for which God be praised. So to prayers and bed.

Samuel Pepys, 23rd February, 1662

Two things fill my mind with ever increasing wonder and awe, the more often and the more intensely the reflection dwells on them: the starry heavens above me and the moral law within me.

Immanuel Kant

Glory be to Thee, O Heavenly Father, for our being and preservation, health and strength, understanding and memory, friends and benefactors, and for all our abilities of mind and body. Glory be to Thee for our competent livelihood, for the advantages of our education, for all known and unobserved deliverances, and for the guard which Thy holy Angels keep over us. Glory be to Thee, O Lord, O Blessed Saviour, for those ordinary gifts by which sincere Christians have in all ages been enabled to work for their salvation, for all the spiritual strength and support, comfort and illumination which we receive from Thee, and for all Thy preserving, restraining and sanctifying grace.

Bishop Thomas Ken

Apologetic Mission

Donald English

Speakers and preachers occasionally find themselves in situations which cause them to question their own sanity in accepting the particular invitation which they find themselves fulfilling. I had one such vivid experience in 1994.

I was leading an evangelistic mission in a college of a large university. We used three major avenues along which to reach the college population.

One was a series of lunchtime seminars. The subjects were Christianity and Politics, Christianity and Science and Christianity and History. Members of staff and students of faculties were invited to the seminar in their own field. A staff member shared with me the initial speaking on the subject and a different chaplain chaired each day. The aim wasn't to preach, or to pronounce on the topic, but rather to share some aspects of a Christian perspective on the particular discipline involved. I tried to pursue a theological line. My co-speaker was invited to take up the subject from within that discipline. Our approach was to pose a question. Does this way of looking at things make sense, and does it have integrity from your point of view as experts or budding experts in the field? We two then engaged in discussion with the chaplain, a discussion which each day was encouraged to develop around the lecture room, which incidentally was full each day.

What interested me first was the level of response. Staff and students came. That was partly because the chaplains had done their work well in approaching departmental heads and communicating the nature of the activity. Secondly, it was fascinating to see how quickly staff and students joined the discussion, once it was clear that we were asking for their views on our perspectives, and not trying to tell them how to think or what to believe. It was also interesting to learn that people from different subjects within a larger discipline said that this was the first opportunity they had had to meet in this cross-subject way. It was clear that the door was open for further experiments of this kind, a door first opened by the care and courtesy of the chaplains.

Each evening we met for a more formal gathering. There was a beautiful art gallery in the college. The department of music is outstanding there, as is the drama school. There is a very accomplished college choir. In a very highly sophisticated cultural setting therefore, (rather at times resembling a salon), we had our evening meetings. There was a variety of music, both vocal and instrumental. There was drama and also testimony and interview. Towards the end I spoke each evening on a parable of Jesus, or a story about him in the Gospels, seeking to show how Christian faith makes sense in today's world and for today's world. The chaplain who was chairing the evening then encouraged people to think further about the experience they'd had, and pointed out that there were 'listeners', (not counsellors), available if people wished them. A good deal of conversation took place each time.

We now come to that part of the mission which I regretted accepting the nearer I got to it! It was the third avenue of approach, and easily the most daunting. The joint Christian student group had managed, with support from the chaplains, to book the Students' Union building for a 'gig'! I encouraged the idea from the beginning of the plans. The nearer it got the more I wondered at my folly in doing so.

The description of the setting needs to be received with that other art gallery setting in mind, where I had felt so much at home. The hall itself was in almost total darkness, apart from the small candles on the round tables scattered across the floor surface. A professional D.J. had been hired, with amplifiers to match. Conversation in a loud shout was the order of the evening. The bar was next to the hall, so people would be moving in and out throughout the evening's activities, as they stocked up their liquid intake.

The organisers, mostly members of the college Christian Union group, had taken a bold step in inviting friends who weren't Christians to play a part in the entertainment. Some of the drama, as a result, had slightly risqué elements. The young woman who sang with a guitar explained that she'd been singing in local clubs and pubs during the vacation, that she wasn't a Christian, but that she respected anyone who had strong convictions, even if she didn't share them. Everything that happened was loud, loud, loud!

I sat there wondering how ever I got myself into this, assuring myself that I'd bitten off more than I could chew this time, and quietly resolving never to let it happen again. There was a large platform at the front, where the drama and music were presented. But at the side there was a smaller platform, bearing a settee and easy chair and piles of cushions, (Michael Barrymore style, I was told), where first the chaplains and then I would be interviewed and then later I would speak.

The interview was certainly different from anything I'd known previously. The attractive young woman student led the conversation as follows. Was it true that I'd been a Flying Officer in the Royal Air Force? Yes, it was. And was it also true that I'd been on the books of Leicester City and Sunderland football clubs? Yes, it was. Then whatever possessed me to leave such exciting and sexy roles to become a Methodist Minister? (Good question!) I explained that my sex life was wholly satisfactory, and that being a Methodist Minister was far from dull! I got a round of applause for that but I had a feeling I still wasn't winning.

The chaplains followed me through the equivalent of sitting in the stocks having things thrown at them. There was more (loud) music. Then it was my turn. The other young woman presenter told people that I was someone to be respected. I had done a lot of good things which deserved attention. In fact I was really a nice man! With that, I was on.

During this entire evening's noisy progress, and particularly while the students presented their music and drama, an interesting development had taken place. We had started the evening with around seventy or eighty people in the room; quite a good number. But as the evening progressed, and there was loud music, and lots of excellent fun and laughter, more and more students made their way in from the bar and stood, drinks in hand, around the back and side walls. By the time it was my turn, there were some four hundred students in the room. No wonder the chairwoman was laying it on thick. I'm sure she feared, as I certainly felt I knew, that at the upstanding of the parson they'd be off!

In the event no-one moved. For nearly forty minutes I spoke of the parable of the Good Samaritan in terms of our modern society, the needs of the world, the opportunities of those who, like themselves, were receiving top education and the cost if they were to take those opportunities up. It all centred in the pattern of Jesus Christ himself in his life, death and resurrection. The rapt attention I received was almost unnerving. I knew that the prayers of those who were there, and of many others around the country, were being answered. I also knew that the risks these young Christians around me had taken (it was the first time they'd ventured like this into the Union) were being honoured by God.

The invitation to spiritual conversation afterwards was offered in a breezier and funnier way than I am accustomed to. It helped that the students available to talk were all wearing their 'Making Sense' (the motto of the mission) T-shirts. The music then broke out again and the 'gig' went on but, as one of the senior organisers said to me as I left later, 'There are conversations going on all over this building about what you said tonight.' The Students' Union official who was on duty asked me if I would come back again sometime. The doorman thanked me for what I'd said.

That's a true story. I have a feeling that it's also a parable. It's about young Christians who risked themselves and their reputations in order to reach others with good news about Jesus. The major activities were all held on other people's natural territory rather than their own. To use an expression of George W. Hunter, they 'played away from home'. The subjects chosen were those determined by the circumstances of those invited, rather than those of the people issuing the invitation. The atmosphere of each meeting was also suited to those who were expected to come. The use as performers of those who didn't share their faith was moving evidence of that commitment.

And the content began where they were. Throughout, the respected and reliable presence of the chaplains was an enormous strength to everyone.

The Christian communication was not preaching or proclaiming (though there is room for that). It was asking questions, offering perspective on modern issues, sharing a journey of trying to make sense of modern life in terms of the ministry of Jesus Christ. In that light people were invited to reflect on their personal lives and commitments. The Christians felt able to encourage their friends to come because they knew they would be quality events. After each meeting there was opportunity for unforced conversation. By the end of the week the Christians were walking taller, and they could carry on from there. Lives had been changed and would continue to be changed. That work has continued, and the different Christian groups are closer together than they have ever been.

If this is one model of mission, one wonders what conclusions might be drawn from it about the witness of the local church?

It is grace that loves God for himself, and our neighbours for God. The consideration of God's goodness and bounty, the experience of those profitable and excellent emanations from him, may be, and most commonly are, the first motive of our love; but when we are once entered, and have tasted the goodness of God, we love the spring for its own excellency, passing from passion to reason, from thanking to adoring, from sense to spirit, from considering ourselves to an union with God; and this is the image and little representation of heaven; it is beatitude in picture, or rather the infancy and beginnings of glory.

Jeremy Taylor, *Of Charity, or the Love of God*

You are wisdom, uncreated and eternal,
The supreme First Cause, above all being,
Sovereign Godhead, sovereign goodness
Watching unseen the God-inspired wisdom of Christian people.
Raise us, we pray, that we may totally respond
To the supreme, unknown, ultimate, and splendid height
Of your words mysterious and inspired.
There God's secret matters lie covered and hidden
Under darkness both profound and brilliant, silent and wise
You make what is ultimate and beyond brightness
Secretly to shine in all that is most dark.
In your way, ever unseen and intangible,
You fill to the full with most beautiful splendour
Those souls who close their eyes that they may see.
And I please, with love that goes on beyond mind
To all that is beyond mind
Seek to gain much for myself through this prayer.

Prayer of St Denis, Cloud of Unknowing

May God give us thankful hearts and keep us in friendship and brotherly love to our lives' end.

Grace of the Merchant Taylors' Company

At times it has happened to me . . . to be conscious of the presence in the Lord of a soul so united to mine that they seemed to be but one. I felt, as it were, a heart of burning coals together with my own heart, or even within it, so that the two were as one heart. And in that soul and heart of fire I knew and recognised the presence of him who fills heaven and earth.

Father Joseph of Montserrat

I have just returned from Plas Power and there I walked with dear Emily through the wood to the bridge, at the very end resting on a camp stool. I fear I shall not be up to such a walk again. It used to be my favourite one which I never missed taking, but old age now creeps on apace and I cannot expect to do as I wont. I am eighty years of age. Oh, how can I reckon up this mighty number of years without thanking the Almighty for having guided me so far under his protection! And for wonderful health, very few grey hairs and sound teeth. To be so old and to feel at the same time so young and susceptible of all the enjoyments of life is tantalising – to see oneself in a looking glass and to think how strange it is that housed within is still that young Welsh girl.

Memoirs of Mary Elizabeth Lucy,
The Mistress of Charlcote

I considered, what difference did I find by an increase in years? I find 1. less activity: I walk slower, particularly uphill: 2. My memory is not so quick: 3. I cannot read so quick by candle light. But I bless God that all my other powers of body and mind remain just as they were.

John Wesley, 1st March, 1788

What we see here of this world is but an expression of God's will, so to speak – a beautiful earth and sky and sea – beautiful affections and sorrows, wonderful changes and developments of creation, suns rising, stars shining, birds singing, clouds and shadows changing and fading, people loving each other, smiling and crying, the multiplied phenomena of Nature, multiplied in fact and fancy, in Art and Science, in every way that a man's intellect or education or imagination can be brought to bear. And who is to say that we are to ignore all this, or not value them and love them, because there is another unknown world yet to come? Why that unknown future world is but a manifestation of God Almighty's will, and a development of Nature, neither more or less than this in which we are, and an angel glorified or a sparrow on a gutter are equally parts of His creation. The light upon all the saints in Heaven is just as much and no more God's work, as the sun which shall shine tomorrow upon this infinitesimal speck of creation.

William Makepeace Thackeray

Oh! I could spend whole days, and moonlight nights, in feeding upon a lovely prospect. My eyes drink the rivers as they flow. If every human being on earth could think for one quarter of an hour, as I have done for many years, there might perhaps be many miserable men among them, but an unawakened one would not be found . . . At present the difference between them and me is greatly to their advantage. I delight in baubles, and know them to be so far viewed without a reference to their author, what is the earth, what are the planets, what is the sun itself, but a bauble? Better for a man never to have seen them, or to see them with the eyes of a brute, unconscious of what he beholds, than not to be able to say, 'The maker of all these wonders is my friend.'

William Cowper to John Newton, 1780

You never enjoy the world aright, till you see how a sand exhibiteth the power and wisdom of God: and prize in everything the service which they do you, by manifesting his glory and goodness to your Soul, far more than the visible beauty on their surface, or the material services they can do your body . . . Your enjoyment of the world is never right, till every morning you awake in Heaven; see yourself in your Father's Palace; and look upon the skies, the earth and the air as Celestial Joys: having such a reverend esteem of all, as if you were among the Angels . . . You never enjoy the world aright, till the sea itself floweth in your veins, till you are clothed with the heavens, and crowned with the stars: and perceive yourself to be the sole heir of the whole world, and more than so, because men are in it who are every one sole heirs as well as you. Till you can sing and rejoice and delight in God, as misers do in gold, and Kings in sceptres, you never enjoy the world.

Thomas Traherne

Earth is crammed with heaven and every
common bush on fire with God.
But only he who sees takes off his shoes, the rest
sit and pluck blackberries.

Elizabeth Barrett Browning

The goodness of God is not so much to be seen in our creation as redemption, not so much that we are his as that nothing can take us out of his hand.

John Donne

You know my veneration for the Book of Psalms, or most of it; but with some half dozen exceptions the Psalms are surely not adequate vehicles of Christian thanksgiving and joy! Upon this deficiency in our service, Wesley and Whitefield seized, and you know it is the hearty congregational singing of Christian hymns which keeps the humbler Methodists together. Luther did as much for the Reformation by his hymns as by his translation of the Bible. In Germany, the hymns are known by heart by every peasant; they advise, they argue from the hymns and every soul in the church praises God like a Christian, with words which are natural and yet sacred to his mind.

Samuel Coleridge, *Table Talk*

For all that God, in mercy, sends:
For health and children, home and friends;
For comfort in the time of need,
For every kindly word and deed,
For happy thoughts and holy talk,
For guidance in our daily walk –
*   For everything give thanks!*

For beauty in this world of ours,
For verdant grass and fragrant flowers,
For songs of birds, for hum of bees,
For the refreshing summer breeze,
For hill and plain, for stream and wood,
For the great ocean's mighty flood –
*   For everything give thanks!*

For the sweet sleep that comes with night,
For the returning morning's light,
For the bright sun that shines on high,
For the stars glittering in the sky,
For these, and everything we see,
O Lord! our hearts we lift to Thee –
*   For everything give thanks!*

Anonymous

We should spend as much time in thanking God for his benefits as we do in asking for them.

St Vincent de Paul

Communicating the Greatest Message in Song

Marilyn Baker

Music is one of the most beautiful ways of communicating the greatest message there has ever been to the people of the world. Like laughter, music can be universally understood, breaking down language, social and environmental barriers. This was illustrated to me in a wonderful way when I visited Poland a few years ago. The majority of those I sang to didn't know English, but through the songs experienced God's love and his word for the first time.

In the Bible there are numerous illustrations of how God used music to influence individuals and situations. Through the Psalms, especially, we can appreciate how musicians and lyricists used their gifts to express understanding of God's word and appreciation of him through praise and worship. There are situations spoken of where music was used to defuse anger, or to undermine the working of evil spirits and forces. Saul was possessed, but his heart was moved by David's playing of the harp.

Many people who will listen to a song wouldn't go to a church service or listen to a preacher. But with ease they will listen to God's word being expressed through music, as they hear a song on the radio, television, or play a tape or CD. So much can be said in a song that cannot be expressed through words alone, since the music is necessary to convey the atmosphere of what is being said and heighten the listener's understanding and appreciation of the true meaning of the words. Music evokes feeling, which mere words cannot.

If you speak the phrase 'God loves you' it can slip off the tongue so easily, sometimes almost glibly, but if the phrase is sung with a poignant melody it can really strike a chord in the heart. Because music penetrates our feelings, moods are influenced and affected by it; joy and warmth as well as pathos can be evoked. I believe, therefore, that music and song are some of God's greatest gifts to us.

When I write I always try to think of the man in the street who may not have had much exposure to Christian literature and jargon – those who may not even own or have had access to a Bible! I am always thrilled when someone, who isn't a church-goer, tells me the songs God's inspired me to write are really helping them. That means I am succeeding in putting deep truths in a simple, straightforward way. My rule of thumb is that if you cannot speak the words easily, if they sound clumsy, then they shouldn't be used in a song. It is also very important for the tune to bring life to the words. If positive thoughts are being expressed, generally the tune should not be in a minor key or drop in a descending scale pattern. The use of ascending, more lively sounding sequences expresses happy moments.

I'm frequently asked what makes a Christian song a 'hit'. In addition to good lyrics, the success of a song depends on having a catchy melody, one that everyone can latch on to! It's not always easy to achieve this. I get a lot of songs sent to me which don't really work. Either the melodies are complicated – which means that if they are sung other than as solos, people will be 'wandering all over the place', or the tunes can be monotonous. I found this a real problem when I first started song-writing.

My harmony professor at the Royal College of Music told me my melodies were boring. Then a girl in my year – Lou Hales (now Lou Lewis) wrote some songs about her new and wonderful relationship with Christ. They buzzed with life and expression. I asked her how she managed to write such wonderful material and she said she had asked the Holy Spirit to inspire her. Although I'd been a Christian for some time I had never thought about God giving anointing for creative gifts like song-writing. I so wanted to communicate my faith. Could God give me his power to write like that? Then I sat down on my bed and quite literally asked him to give me new ideas for interesting and inspiring melodies – the weak point in my song-writing. I asked for the ability to put together words and music that would reveal and express his heart. It was a big prayer to pray and I must say that I didn't know then the implications of it for my future! But God is utterly faithful and from that time onwards new ideas began to come.

The first song I wrote, 'He's my Saviour, my friend and my Lord', was composed especially to sing at a weekly meeting I was leading for my College Christian Union. This song had a great beat, quite a black Gospel feel to it. We were more used to singing pieces from oratorios, so we had to change our style a bit, but it was very exciting and exhilarating as we got into the swing. The kids loved it and my College friends kept urging me to do more. But nothing came for a long time – not until I moved to Watford two years later. The lesson here was not to try to force the inspiration. Nothing is worth writing unless it is anointed. God needs to be the author and creator of his songs, as all things. His anointing provides the creative source, to use one's thoughts and style effectively. The best songs, like the best stories, come from one's own experience of everyday life. There is a truthfulness which shines from songs resulting from personal experience, from what one has felt deep inside.

Music is a wonderful medium to communicate God's truths. This was brought home to me early in my song-writing when I went with friends to sing in a local pub. I would take my squeeze-box and sing the customers' favourite songs. These were not Christian songs, but we were 'bridge building'. One night I returned home and had a longing to communicate something about God's love to these people. I began to 'feel' their emptiness and confusion about life and to see their need to know God's love and acceptance and understand his nature. The result was, 'God wants to give you a glorious new life that can satisfy, that will never die. His life will change you and set your heart free, to be all that God intends you to be.'

On another occasion, I was walking down Watford High Street and a phrase with the beginning of a tune kept going through my mind – 'Jesus, you are changing me.' I recoiled at the idea of writing a song that seemed so positive. The next day I came across 2 Corinthians 3, which speaks about us being changed into his likeness by the power of the Holy Spirit. I realised God was talking to me and encouraging me to put his words into a song.

He seemed to ask me whether I believed my feelings more than his word and told me that though I may not think I was being changed his Spirit was doing this work within me. By the end of the week I was convinced that, though I had a long way to go, God had started to do a deep work in my life. I then wrote this chorus now sung in many churches, which has encouraged so many to believe in his changing power.

More often than not, the songs I write minister to me first. By nature I am a worrier. One day I was travelling to a friend's house; I had to get two buses and, being blind I feared I may not know when the second bus was coming and get on the wrong one. I had a guide dog who went everywhere with me, but I had to ask people the right way to go places and often I became very anxious. The Lord seemed to speak to my anxiety and assure me of his presence and help with the words 'rest in my love', and a song which helped me and many others since was born.

This song ends, 'You are my child and I care for you, there's nothing my power and love cannot do.' I hope those reading this article who have a desire to write songs will be inspired to 'have a go'! It may be they will never write a 'hit', but one thing is certain, God will speak to them through the experience and may show them other ways to communicate his love to others, or heighten their appreciation of his message through music.

But wouldst thou know the beauty of holiness? Go alone on some week day, borrowing the keys of good Master Sexton, traverse the cool aisles of some country church; think of the piety that has kneeled there, the congregations old and young, that have found consolation there – the meek pastor – the docile parishioner. With no disturbing emotions, no cross comparisons, drink in the tranquillity of the place, till thou thyself become as fixed and motionless as the marble effigies which kneel and weep around thee.

Charles Lamb, *Essays of Elia*

Thanks be to thee, my joy and my glory and my confidence, my God, thanks be to thee for thy gifts; do thou preserve them to me. For so wilt thou preserve me, and those things shall be enlarged and perfected which thou hast given me, and I myself shall be with thee, since thou hast given me to exist.

St Augustine, Confessions

God is actively present in each tiny human event persuading us by loving visions to transform ourselves continually. God is one of our constant relationships. God is in the midst of our deepest processes. Like one unique voice in a choir, one special instrument in an orchestra that blends with the many others, God is present persuading the many to become one in beauteous harmony.

Robert Brizee, *Where in the World is God?*

Glory be to God for dappled things –
  For skies of couple-colour as a brinded cow;
For rose-moles all in stipple upon trout that swim;
  Fresh firecoal chestnut-falls; finches' wings;
Landscapes plotted and pieced – fold, fallow and plough;
  And all trades, their gear and tackle and trim.

All things counter, original, spare, strange;
  Whatever is fickle, freckled (who knows how?)
With swift, slow; sweet, sour; adazzle, dim;
  He fathers-forth whose beauty is past change:
  Praise him.

Gerard Manley Hopkins, Pied Beauty

This day His Majesty Charles II came to London after a sad and long exile and calamitous suffering both of the king and church, being seventeen years. This was also his birthday and with a triumph of above 20,000 horse and foot, brandishing their swords and shouting with inexpressible joy: the way strewed with flowers, the bells ringing, the streets hung with tapestry, fountains running with wine . . . I stood in the Strand and beheld it and blessed God. And all this was done without one drop of blood shed, and by that very army which rebelled against him: but it was the Lord's doing, for such a restoration was never mentioned in any history ancient or modern, since the return of the Jews from the Babylonish captivity: nor so joyful a day and so bright ever seen in this nation, this happening when to expect or to effect it was past all human policy.

John Evelyn, *Diary*, 29th May, 1660

I love all beauteous things
I seek and adore them;
God hath no better praise.
And man in his hasty days
Is honoured for them.

I too will make something
And joy in the making;
Altho' tomorrow it seem
Like the empty words of a dream
Remembered on waking.

Robert Bridges, All Beauteous Things

Sunrise is an event that calls forth solemn music in the very depths of man's nature, as if one's whole being had to attune itself to the cosmos and praise God for the new day, praise him in the name of all the creatures that ever were or ever will be. I look at the rising sun and feel that now upon me falls the responsibility of seeing what all my ancestors have seen, in the Stone Age and ever before it, praising God before me. Whether or not they praised him then, for themselves, they must praise him now in me. When the sun rises each one of us is summoned by the living and the dead to praise God.

Thomas Merton, *Conjectures of a Guilty Bystander*

Now that the daylight fills the sky,
We lift our hearts to God on high,
That He, in all we do or say,
Would keep us free from harm today:

Would guard our hearts and tongues from strife;
From anger's din would hide our life:
From all ill sights would turn our eyes,
Would close our ears from vanities.

So we, when this new day is gone,
And night in turn is drawing on,
With conscience by the world unstained
Shall praise His name for victory gained.

All laud to God the Father be;
All praise, eternal Son, to Thee;
All glory, as is ever meet,
To God the holy Paraclete.

Office Hymn for Prime

Let us not then deem God inferior to human workmen, who, in proportion to their skill finish and perfect their works, small as well as great, by one and the same art; or that God, the wisest of beings, who is both willing and able to care, is like a lazy good-for-nothing who turns his back upon labour and gives no thought to smaller and easier matters, but to the greater only.

Plato

Let my soul be a mirror that will reflect thee to the world.
Live thou in my thought.
Live thou in my speech.
Live thou in all my deeds.
O most Holy.

Prayer of Narayan Vaman Marathi, Christian poet

The Black Mountains were invisible, being wrapped in clouds, and I saw one very bright, brilliant dazzling cloud where the mountains ought to have been. This cloud grew more white and dazzling every moment, till a clearer burst of sunlight scattered the mists and revealed the truth. The brilliant white cloud that I had been looking at and wondering at was the mountain in snow. The last cloud and mist rolled away over the mountain tops and the mountain stood up in the clear blue heaven, a long rampart line of dazzling glittering snow so as no fuller on earth can whiten them. I stood rooted to the ground, struck with amazement and overwhelmed at the extraordinary splendour of this marvellous spectacle. I never saw anything to equal it, I think, even among the high Alps. One's first involuntary thought is to lift up the heart to God and humbly thank him for having made the earth so beautiful.

Kilvert's Diary, 14th March, 1871

Look around us, who created these
Sun, moon, stars and the earth which smiles so fair?
They whirl through space, held there by his word
While he leans on Mary's gentle breast.

The boy who was born, but a span's length at birth
Is the Son whose span measures the whole world,
A tiny babe on his mother's breast
And yet able to support the whole universe safely.

Nineteenth century Welsh carol

A low prayer, a high prayer, I send through space,
Arrange them Thyself, O Thou King of Grace.

Irish Prayer

Praise above all – for praise prevails
Heap up the measure, load the scales,
And good to goodness add:
The gen'rous soul her Saviour aids
But peevish obloquy degrades
The Lord is great and glad.

Christopher Smart, *A Song to David*

> *Now must we praise the Warden of Heaven's realm*
> *The Creator's might and his mind's thought,*
> *The glorious works of the Father;*
> *How of ever wonder*
> *He, the Lord, the eternal, laid the foundation.*
> *He shaped erst, for the sons of men,*
> *Heaven as their roof, Holy Creator,*
> *The middle world he, mankind's Warden,*
> *Eternal Lord, afterwards prepared*
> *The earth for men, Lord Almighty.*
>
> *Song of Caedmon, seventh century*

Stir up your hearts in an especial manner to the greatest Alacrity and Joy in speaking and singing the Praises of God. The Lord's Day is a day of Joy and Thanksgiving; and the Praises of God are the highest and holiest employment upon earth; and if ever you should do anything with all your might, and with a joyful and triumphing frame of soul, it is this. Be glad that you may join with the sacred assemblies in heart and voice in so heavenly a work.

Richard Baxter, from *The Church Directory*, 1672

The Way of Holiness

William Watty

Few passages of Wesley's writings have afforded me greater pleasure than an extract which was included in Frederick Gill's anthology *Through the Year with Wesley*. John Wesley, it seems, was answering some critics who had been castigating the Methodists for their obsession with holiness:

> 'In God's name,' he asks, 'why are you so fond of sin? What good has it ever done you? What good is it ever likely to do you either in this world or in the world to come? And why are you so violent against us who hope for a deliverance from it? Have patience with us.'
>
> (Upper Room, 1983, pp.30-31)

It is a paragraph that still reads well and should continue to be read by Methodists so long as holiness continues to be the most maligned, best hated, least understood word in the vocabulary of Christian spirituality. 'Holiness' still conjures up negative images by which few Methodists would wish to be identified – narrowness, censoriousness, priggishness, sourness, bigotry. It connotes a super-morality which breeds self-righteousness and complacency on the one hand and disdain and aloofness on the other, and so unattractive and unpopular has the stereotype become, that it is unlikely that a high concentration of Methodists will be found anywhere in the world who would either be thrilled or eager to be recognised as 'holy'.

And yet this, we have been assured, is the *grand depositum* of Methodism. For this purpose, primarily, God in his providence has raised us up – to spread scriptural holiness throughout the world. Here lies the peculiar genius which justifies and validates our continued existence as a Christian communion. It suggests that Methodists, above all other believers, are taking the promises and demands of their faith with a radical seriousness, that they are in a covenant-relationship which assumes a renunciation of all forms of idolatry, complacency and self-deception in a total consecration to God. For Methodists to be indifferent to the quest for holiness or offended by the call to holiness is therefore a crisis of mammoth dimensions which it would be fatal to ignore. An understanding of holiness which would clarify its meaning, and restore the practice to prominence in Methodist spirituality, is therefore urgently required.

That is why I have found Wesley's sharp rejoinder to be so refreshing. With one swift stroke he has cut through all the squeamishness and humbug and stated the issue with such simplicity and candour as even a child might understand. What is so dangerous about holiness that it must be pursued clandestinely, so to speak? And what is so marvellous about sin that a mere call to renounce it must inflame such animosity? And why must Methodists apologise for wishing to be free from its taint and power? Give us a break!

Unfortunately, the clarity and vigour which typified Wesley's writings did not rub off on his successors, and those who knew him best and venerated him to the point of hagiography did not learn from him that useful art. It might have kept Methodism, on both sides of the Atlantic, on an even keel even as it grew by leaps and bounds. Instead, clarity of thinking, in the period following Wesley's demise, showed not so much a decline as a drop, and nowhere was muddled

thinking so widespread and so evident in the
understanding, the quest, the experience and the
practice of Christian holiness.

Let it be noted, however, that even in Wesley's lifetime
a problem existed. Wesley's soteriology was
complicated by a defective anthropology. The problem
is laid bare in José Miguez Bonino's contribution to the
collection of essays on *Sanctification and Liberation*
(Ed. T. Runyon). Bonino examines Wesley's doctrine
of sanctification from a liberationist perspective, and
while he gives due credit to Wesley's special and
primary emphasis on sanctification as a force for
upward social mobility (Abingdon, ibid p.53) he also
detects a serious flaw in Wesley's perception of the
person who is called to and seeks after holiness.
Bonino contends:

> Wesley's anthropology seems to me to be
> incurably individualistic. This criticism may
> appear arbitrary in the light of the repeated
> assertions concerning the social character of the
> Christian life, his insistence on 'a social
> holiness', his indictment of 'a solitary religion',
> and his practical arrangements to ensure a
> corporate growth in faith and holiness. A
> careful exegesis of the contexts in which these
> expressions occur will show, I believe, that for
> Wesley, society is not an anthropological
> concept, but simply a convenient arrangement
> for the growth of the individual. It is the
> individual soul that is finally saved, sanctified
> and perfected. The fellowship is, in the last
> instance, an *externum subidium* ... It is not to be
> despised or neglected ... But still man is a soul
> in terms of both eschatological hope and
> religious experience. The drama of justification
> and sanctification takes place in the subjectivity

of the inner life although it seeks objective
expression in works of love.   (ibid p.55)

The criticism is not intended in any way to be a
disparagement of Wesley's substantial contribution to
the understanding and promotion of Christian
spirituality. It is simply a salutary reminder that
Wesley was a child of his age, and that it was pre-
eminently an age of Reason over which the strong
Cartesian individualism and egocentricity, 'I think,
therefore, I am,' held sway. Sociology and
anthropology as exact sciences, and their
interrelationship, had not yet emerged. The individual
was perceived as an autonomous entity over against
and distinguishable from another alien entity called
'society'. Conceivably, therefore, an individual could
attain the perfection of holiness in complete separation
from his social context, and it is precisely here that the
weakness of Wesley's position lay.

Doubtless, Wesley deserves high commendation for
following his social instincts to the point of frustrating
the individualistic logic of his own doctrine of
salvation. He rejected firmly the solitary religion to
which it tended and accentuated social responsibility
as proof of holiness when, in fact, such a responsibility
did not logically derive from his understanding of
either justification or sanctification. Charles Wesley
could write:

> Not in the tombs we pine to dwell,
> Not in the dark monastic cell,
>   By vows and grates confined,
> Freely ourselves to all we give,
> Constrained by Jesu's love to live,
>   The servants of mankind.

But, unlike Isaiah, he could participate in a society of
'people of unclean lips' and still not be a 'man of

unclean lips' (Isaiah 6:5). It was this dichotomy at the heart of Wesley's understanding of sanctification, this hiatus between the individual and the social group to which he/she might belong, which oversimplified his understanding of the human predicament, reduced the dimensions of salvation and left the door open to the distortions and wild excesses which poured in like a flood after his death.

The tragic paradox was that in the 19th and the early 20th centuries, the balanced view of holiness which Wesley bequeathed was capsized by his followers who took his teaching to its logical conclusion. They marginalised the emphasis on social responsibility, privatised and sensationalised what remained into promises of a 'second blessing', revivalism, ecstatic experiences and other similar charismatic excesses, and trivialised the ethical and social thrust into a new legalism of prohibitions – 'touch not, taste not, handle not' (Colossians 2:21).

The major debate taking place today across all the denominations is precisely about that dualism, that dichotomy and that hiatus which pretend to separate the inner life from the outer and the individual from the social group, for there is in fact no hiatus, no dichotomy, no dualism. The holy person whom God sees is not the inner soul but the whole person who 'dwells in the midst of a people . . .' and is authentically related to that society. The reality of social solidarity is inescapable for the correct understanding of salvation whether in terms of repentance, faith or holiness. Anything else and anything less is ingenious escapism and a sham. There is no human being who is not a historical being in the sense that his/her historical situation inevitably impinges upon his/her inner condition and spirituality and is in turn affected by the decisions he/she takes or fails or refuses to take. That is where the quest for holiness begins because that is how God made us and where it has pleased God to place us. There, in the totality of our being, and in conscious, practical solidarity with our fellow human beings God waits to meet us and there we shall see God. That is holiness.

Even the horizontal/vertical approach is an unsatisfactory way of expressing the reality and is, in a sense, both mistaken and misleading, for it preserves the dualism. The dichotomy persists with all its potential for a holiness which is characterised by social indifference beyond the circle of home and family, and complacency about social wrongs even when they have become entrenched in the home and in the heart. Such a holiness is a caricature and an alibi for that callous abdication of responsibility which prophet after prophet brought under heavy indictment.

Ever since the Bethlehem-event the vertical has become an horizontal, historical phenomenon. 'The Word was made flesh and dwelt among us' (John 1:14). Therefore it is only as flesh, in historical decisions and historical actions, here and now, that we can become part of and participants in the divine project. Repentance – the porch of religion, faith – the door of religion, and holiness – religion itself, must be understood, practised and celebrated in that context, otherwise they are alibis and attempts at covering up something else. Does it mean, then, that we do not pray or worship? Does it mean that we must abolish festivals and fasts? Does it mean that we must turn our backs on liturgies and mysteries and no longer sing the hymns, the canticles and the psalms? Of course not. But what it does mean is that none of these events, activities or observances can ever be de-historicised. For better or for worse they contribute positively or negatively to the maturity of the human being as a social and historical being. They are either ingredients of or deterrents to social change and development.

JOY
&
SERENITY

*Whatever is to make us better
and happy, God has placed either
openly before us or close to us.*

Seneca

Doves are flying in my garden,
Soft wings brushing cool grey stone.
They pass in and out
Of golden light and deep green shade
As pleased with both,
So long as still sweet water lies
Around the mossy fountain.

Dear Lord, and even so may I
In this, the garden of my life
Go out and in
Through sun and shadow,
For my part content as they,
Because the still sweet water of Your Love
Unfailing, feeds the channels of my heart.

Dorothy Elgar

By six I came to Epworth, my native place. All who met me saluted me with hearty joy. At eight I preached, in Edward Smith's yard. 'He that spared not his own Son' etc. Many were present and much affected. I laid me down in peace, after one of the happiest days I have ever known.

Charles Wesley, 22nd June, 1743

Joy and Serenity

Michael Saward

'Oh joy, oh rapture unforeseen, for now the sky is all serene.' So I sang as a sixteen-year-old sailor in the chorus of *H.M.S. Pinafore*. Well, that's how teenagers see the world today and by tomorrow they will be echoing Ralph Rackstraw's sad farewell, 'My friends, my leave of life I'm taking, for oh, my heart, my heart is breaking.' Except, of course, that it's the other way round in *Pinafore*. As it often is in life. Joy and grief, serenity and heartache. And for all those whose lives are dedicated to caring, the strange experience of relating to first one, and then the other. Clergy and ministers are peculiarly caught up in the task of 'weeping with those who weep' and 'rejoicing with those who rejoice'. In its most extreme form it happens when you conduct a funeral and a wedding on the same day.

So what about joy? What is it? According to the Oxford English Dictionary it is a 'pleasurable emotion due to well-being or satisfaction', and this definition is coupled with 'the feeling or state of being highly pleased', 'exultation of spirit', 'gladness and delight'. All of which sounds to be very enjoyable, and I'll get Fortnum and Mason to deliver ten tons of it tomorrow morning.

The only problem with that kind of definition is that it comes perilously close to the attitude of the man referred to by Jesus in one of his parables, the man who had been a great business success with his bigger and better granaries and who urged himself to 'take life easy; eat, drink, and enjoy yourself.' He certainly had 'pleasurable emotion due to well-being or satisfaction' but he was, said Jesus, about to die and lose it all for he was 'a pauper in the sight of God'.

So there's got to be more to joy than comfort and success. 'Comfort and Success' are, like 'Triumph and Disaster', in Kipling's poem *If*, two impostors. Neither pair brings joy, real joy, as a guaranteed prospect. Joy doesn't 'come up with the rations'.

So, again, we ask, what is joy? Schiller tells us, in words made doubly famous by Beethoven's setting in his *Choral Symphony*, that Joy (Freude) is:

schöner Götterfunken, tochter aus Elysium

which, in translation, personalises her as:

beautiful radiance of the gods, daughter of heaven

under whose tender wing:

alle Menschen werden Brüder.

Well, it all sounds warming to the heart to be told that 'all men become brothers' under Joy's wing, but the unromantic among us have inspected history too closely to believe that the dream ever comes true outside the pages of sentimental poetry.

Oh dear, that sounds like a 'no hope' situation, doesn't it?

Of course, we could turn to the Bible. The 'joy' words (there are, broadly, three) keep popping up there. Perhaps a quick glance won't hurt us. And, just to be sure that my source is properly kosher, I've drawn heavily on a massive work described by the *Methodist Recorder* as 'fully comprehensive and of an extremely high standard of scholarship'. The article on 'Joy' in Volume Two of the *New International Dictionary of New Testament Theology* helpfully sets out the three words.

Let's take first *euphraino*. Its essential characteristic is 'the subjective feeling of joy'. This can be either good or bad and Luke, especially, uses the word of convivial merriment coupled with some celebration. It may be the joy at the feast given to mark the return of the Prodigal Son; it may be that of the Rich Fool's planned party or the riotous and idolatrous orgy marking the worship of the golden bull-calf made by Aaron at Mount Sinai. One valuable lesson comes to us from *euphraino* and that is that the experience of 'joy' is, in itself, morally neutral. Relying on the fact that one feels 'joyfully high' is no guarantee of the validity of the feeling. It's hardly surprising, then, that St. Paul very rarely uses the word when he wants to encourage Christians to be joyful.

The second word is *agalliaomai*. Here the essential idea is 'the outward demonstration of joy'. It's a noisy, jubilant word and is the mark of a church and people who are thrilled to be participating in the new, eschatological age of salvation inaugurated by Jesus of Nazareth. It looks ahead to the worship of heaven and the heavenly banquet, and it does so by eucharistic worship 'with unaffected joy', as one of the more formal modern translations puts it. I live and work in one of the world's great Cathedrals and the music is magnificent and superb. The liturgy is beautifully choreographed and thousands of people come Sunday by Sunday. That said, I often wonder what would happen if such worship had the added element of 'noisy, unaffected jubilation'. I suspect that some of the traditionalists would have a fit. Such people talk about 'celebrating the eucharist' but they use the word 'celebrate' in a way that wouldn't ring any bells with the way the general public understands 'celebration'.

The final word is *chairo* and it is the key word in the New Testament's understanding of 'joy'. The first two are to be found only thirty times. The third is used one hundred and thirty-three times. The first two are about feelings and outward expressions. *Chairo* is much deeper than that. *Chairo* (and its noun, *Chara*) are concerned with the underlying sense of being secure in Christ. To know him, to know what he has done for me, to know his purposes for his people – this is joy in its most profound form. Moreover, this kind of joy remains, come hell or high water, and the apostles encourage Christ's followers to be 'joyful in tribulation', to bear 'long-suffering with joy', knowing that Christ did just that on the cross.

Serenity isn't a New Testament word as such but that is exactly what *chara* is. It is joy, deep-rooted, peaceful, of the kind Martin Luther knew when he wrote:

> And though they take our life
> goods, honour, children, wife,
> yet is their profit small;
> these things shall vanish all;
> the City of God remaineth.

Put in a vivid way, E. Stanley Jones, the American Methodist missionary in India, once said that, 'when I met Christ, I felt that I had swallowed sunshine', while another, anonymous writer described joy as 'the royal standard floating from the flagstaff of the heart, telling us that the King is in residence'.

But does it work? Nearly a decade ago, three men broke into my Vicarage in Ealing, raped my daughter Jill, and fractured my skull with one of my cricket bats. In a televised interview in hospital I said, a week later, that it had been 'the most wonderful week of my life ... the culmination of my ministry'. Was I mad, deranged, soft in the head? Had I no feelings for my ravished, buggered daughter? The world simply couldn't understand. But we knew, Jill and I, that despite the grief and sense of shame which she would bear (and has long since, thank God, overcome), we knew that our hope and trust in Christ had faced the test, the 'time of trial', and that we were not destroyed but strengthened and upheld. And the sense of joy, in the midst of pain, was the living proof of a Saviour who had borne our griefs and carried our sorrows.

'Joy to the world,' wrote Isaac Watts, 'the Lord has come.' 'Amen to that,' say I.

Life is not made up of great sacrifices and duties but of little things: in which smiles and kindness given habitually are what win and preserve the heart and secure comfort.

Sir Humphrey Davy

I heard a voice which said, 'There is one, even Jesus Christ, that can speak to thy condition,' and when I heard it, my heart did leap for joy.

George Fox

When I woke again many of the stars had disappeared: only the stronger companions of the night still burned visibly overhead: and away toward the east I saw a faint haze of light upon the horizon, such as had been the Milky Way when I was last awake. Day was at hand . . . The blue darkness lay long in the glade where I had so sweetly slumbered: but soon there was a broad streak of orange melting into gold along the mountain tops of Vivarais. A solemn glee possessed my mind at this gradual and lovely coming in of day. I heard the runnel with delight: I looked round me for something beautiful and unexpected: but the still black pine trees, the hollow glade, the munching ass, remained unchanged in figure. Nothing had altered but the light, and that, indeed, shed over all a spirit of life and of breathing peace, and moved me to a strange exhilaration.

Robert Louis Stevenson, *Travels with a Donkey*

It is true we cannot judge of ourselves by the measure of our joy; the most variable of all our sensations, and frequently depending in a great degree on the state of our blood and spirits. But if you take love, joy, peace, meekness, gentleness and resignation together, I know of no rule surer whereby to judge your state to God-ward.

John Wesley, 15th September, 1770

True happiness, we are told, consists in getting out of one's self, but the point is not only to get out – you must stay out: and to stay out you must have some absorbing errand.

Henry James, *Roderick Hudson*

You are lucky. You are always so even and untroubled; it sometimes seems to me that you are unaffected by any separations, feelings and changes. This is not because of any frigidity in your nature, or from indifference, but there is something in you which does not allow you to attach importance to the things of everyday life.

Letter from Olga Chekhov to her husband, Anton

The glory of a good man is the testimony of a good conscience. Have a good conscience and thou shalt ever have joy. A good conscience is able to bear very much, and is cheerful in adversities. An evil conscience is always fearful and unquiet. Thou shalt rest sweetly, if thy heart do not reprehend thee. Never rejoice but when thou hast done well.

Thomas à Kempis, The Imitation of Christ

O God, make us children of quietness and heirs of peace.

St Clement

He said the pleasantest manner was spending a hot July day lying from morning till evening on a bank of heath in the middle of the moors, with the bees humming dreamily about among the bloom, and the larks singing high up overhead, and the blue sky and bright sun shining steadily and cloudlessly. That was his most perfect idea of heaven's happiness; mine was rocking in a rustling green tree, with a west wind blowing, and bright white clouds flitting rapidly above; and not only larks, but throstles, and blackbirds, and linnets, and cuckoos pouring music on every side, and the moors seen at a distance, broken into cool dusky dells; but close by great swells of long grass undulating in waves to the breeze; and woods and sounding water, and the whole world awake and wild with joy. He wanted all to lie in an ecstasy of peace; I wanted all to sparkle and dance in a glorious jubilee.

Emily Brontë, *Wuthering Heights*

When from our better selves we have too long
Been parted by the hurrying world, and droop
Sick of its business, of its pleasures tired,
How gracious, how benign is solitude;
How potent a mere image of her sway;
Most potent when impressed upon the mind
With an appropriate human centre – hermit
Deep in the bosom of the wilderness
Votary (in vast cathedral where no foot
Is treading, where no other face is seen)
Kneeling at prayers; or watchman on the top
Of lighthouse, beaten by Atlantic waves;
Or as the soul of that great Power is met
Sometimes embodied on a public road,
When, for the night deserted, it assumes
A character of quiet more profound
Than pathless wastes.

William Wordsworth, from The Prelude

There lives no man on earth who may always have rest and peace without troubles and crosses, with whom things go always according to his will. There is always something to be suffered here, consider it as you will. Seek only that true peace of the heart, which none can take away from you, that you may overcome all adversity; the peace that breaks through all adversities and crosses, all oppression, suffering, misery, humiliation, and what more there may be of the like, so that a man may be joyful and patient therein. Now if a man were lovingly to give his whole diligence and might thereto, he could very soon come to know that true eternal peace which is God Himself, as far as it is possible to a creature; insomuch that his heart would remain ever unmoved among all things.

Theologia Germanica

In the woods a man casts off his years, as the snake his slough, and what period soever of his life, is always a child. In the woods is perpetual youth. Within these plantations of God, a decorum and sanctity reign, a perennial festival is dressed, and the guest sees not how he should tire of them in a thousand years. In the woods we return to reason and faith. There I feel that nothing can befall me in life – no disgrace, no calamity which nature cannot repair. Standing on the bare ground – my head bathed by the blithe air, and uplifted into infinite space – all mean egotism vanishes.

Ralph Waldo Emerson, *Nature*

More than Champions

Kriss Akabusi

At the first warm weather training camp in my athletics career, in Bolzano in the Northern Italian Alps in 1979, I picked up a quote from Alexander Pope, the English poet from the Age of Reason: 'Blessed are they who expect nothing for they will not be disappointed.' I wrote this down in my training diary and determined that this would be my approach to winning in athletics. So I began my track and field career. Train, compete and be happy. 'Laissez-faire' must rule the day. So it did; within five years I was competing at the highest level a sportsman can achieve – the Olympic Games.

Pierre de Coubertin, the founder of the modern Olympic Games, seemed to amplify Pope's precept when he said, 'The important thing in the Olympic Games is not to win, but to take part; the important thing in life is not the triumph but the struggle; the essential thing is not having conquered but to have fought well.'

However I was soon to learn the folly of these words in the modern era. I won a silver medal in the British relay quartet and made the semi-final as an individual. I certainly had not expected the silver and had only hoped that I would make the semis. I was ecstatic with jubilation. On my return home I was to learn from experience a cruel truth. In world class sport, winning is everything. Coming second means nothing. Marketing managers and public relations officers want winners; sponsors and advertisers want winners;

armchair critics and enthusiastic punters want winners. 'Win, win, win,' say the media moguls, 'and we will make you stars.' Sport, it seemed, was definitely more than a game.

Eight years later, I was to be in my third Olympic Games. As European and Commonwealth Champion in my own right and World Champion with the aid of my relay colleagues, I went to the games with one thing on my mind – 'Champion Olympique'. I was not in my best physical shape but mentally I was prepared. I feared none of my competitors but respected them all. You have to be good to make an Olympic final, and I was up against the world's greatest.

As I blasted from my blocks I felt fine and things were going great until halfway round. Then Kevin Young, a hitherto unheralded outsider from the USA, came blowing past me between hurdles three and four; by hurdle five he was a full five metres up, not including the stagger. My dream was becoming a nightmare. A bad one! I kept on working hard. Into the home straight and there was still something to run for – only Kevin and Winthrop Graham were ahead of me, albeit eight metres in Kevin's case. Blam! I crossed the line and the big screen flashed, 'Kevin Young – New world record!' Kevin had just become the fastest man in history. Back in third place I once again became the fastest man in British history. At that moment I learnt a lesson that would stay with me the rest of my life: I was never going to be Olympic Champion.

For many people, an Olympic medal of any description will be beyond their wildest dreams. But one thing that Kevin and I had in common that day was that we had both given of our very best effort. My time and position represented the very best that I could be on that day. That is something that we can *all* aspire to.

To do whatever we choose, to the best of our ability, and in so doing to be content. Both Pope and de Coubertin were right: aspire to many things, expect nothing, fight, struggle and play to win, but not at all costs; for sport, after all, should be no more than a game.

Becoming a Christian changed my attitude to athletics. Before I was a Christian I felt that I was only as good as my last race. If I ran badly I was a nobody. As a Christian I came to realise that I could glorify God no matter where I finished. I realised that God had given me the ability and it was just up to me to do my best. If I was to win that was good but if I was to come last, 'C'est la vie.'

I still want to win and want to do my best. By winning I can bring glory to God – but I can also glorify God if I don't win.

In the 1992 Olympics, I was just as hungry as anyone and I wanted to win an Olympic gold medal. I thought I could do it. Coming third was a real disappointment, but I was still able to give thanks to God for his goodness in getting me there. Being a Christian helped me to accept the achievement of coming third and keep it in perspective.

Crossing the finishing line first and being the best we can be are not the same thing.

Best of all, in God's eyes, we can never lose.

I've always dreamed of solitude, the hermit's life, a cabin in the woods or a tiny chalet on the edge of a mountain. I've always dreamed of deserts and silence. But I've resisted the dream, with the exception of one time when I offered myself the luxury of a retreat with a hermit: four hours by foot, far from any living creature and a hermit happy to see me. We talked a lot.

Michel Quoist, *With Open Heart*

Today

Mend a quarrel. Search out a forgotten friend. Dismiss suspicion and replace it with trust. Write a love letter. Share some treasure. Give a soft answer. Encourage youth. Manifest your loyalty in a word or deed.

Keep a promise. Find the time. Forego a grudge. Forgive an enemy. Listen. Apologise if you were wrong. Try to understand. Flout envy. Examine your demands on others. Think first of someone else. Appreciate, be kind, be gentle. Laugh a little more.

Deserve confidence. Take up arms against malice. Decry complacency. Express your gratitude. Worship God. Gladden the heart of a child. Take pleasure in the beauty and wonder of the earth. Speak your love. Speak it again. Speak it still again. Speak it still once again.

Author unknown

I know well that happiness is in little things if anywhere, but it is essentially within one, and being within seems to fasten on little things. When I have been unhappy, I have heard an opera from end to end and it seemed the shrieking of winds; when I am happy, a sparrow's chirp is delicious to me. But it is not the chirp that makes me happy, but that I make it sweet.

John Ruskin

Hence the reason why almost all men, and those that seem to be very miserable, love life, because they cannot bear to lose sight of such a beautiful and lovely world. The ideas that every moment whilst we live have a beauty that we take not distinct notice of, bring a pleasure that, when we come to the trial, we had rather live in much pain and misery than lose.

Jonathan Edwards, *The Beauty of the World*

It was a fine day, and the crowds of people exceeded what I have ever seen; many as there were the day I went into the City, it was nothing – nothing to the multitudes, the millions of my loyal subjects who were assembled in every spot to witness the Procession. Their good humour and excessive loyalty was beyond everything, and I really cannot say how proud I am to be the Queen of such a Nation.

Queen Victoria, *Diary*, 28th June, 1838

May the road
rise up to meet you.
May the wind
be always at your back.
May the sun shine
warm upon your face,
The rains
fall soft upon the fields
And until we meet again
May you be held
in the hollow of God's hand.

Traditional Gaelic blessing

Give me the clear blue sky over my head and the green turf beneath my feet, a winding road before me, and a three hours march to dinner – and then to thinking! It is hard if I cannot start some game on these lone heaths. I laugh, I run, I leap, I sing for joy.

William Hazlitt, quoted by Robert Louis Stevenson

'There is a place of quiet rest,' the poet Cleland McAfee wrote, 'near to the heart of God. A place where sin cannot molest.' It can be a place to meet the One whom Helmut Thielike called *The Waiting Father*. No one can live well without such places; but many try.

Gordon MacDonald, *Restoring Your Spiritual Passion*

He that is down needs fear no fall,
He that is up no pride;
He that is humble ever shall have God
To be his guide.

I am content with what I have,
Little be it or much;
And, Lord, contentment still I crave
Because Thou savest such.

Fullness to such a burden is
That go on pilgrimage;
Here little — and hereafter bliss,
Is best from age to age.

John Bunyan, The Shepherd's Song

The great joys of my life have arrived unbidden. The more I sought happiness, the more it eluded me. The more I have snatched at passing happinesses, the more in retrospect have they seemed unsatisfying. But when the need of someone else or of a group of people has wrenched me out of my cocoon, then even in the midst of terrifying anxiety, stress and fatigue, I have found a surpassing joy which has somehow taken me by the scruff of my neck!

Frank Collier, *The Parables of Jesus*

Take time to laugh
It is the music of the soul.

Take time to think
It is the source of power.

Take time to play
It is the source of perpetual youth.

Take time to read
It is the fountain of wisdom.

Take time to pray
It is the greatest power on earth.

Take time to love and be loved
It is a God-given privilege.

Take time to be friendly
It is the road to happiness.

Take time to give
It is too short a day to be selfish.

Take time to work
It is the price of success.

Anonymous

Feel Free

Ann Bird

One day people will touch and talk perhaps easily,
And loving be natural as breathing and warm as
  sunlight,
And people will untie themselves, as string is
  unknotted,
Unfold and yawn and stretch and spread their
  fingers,
Unfurl, uncurl like seaweed returned to the sea,
And work will be simple and swift as a seagull
  flying,
And play will be casual and quiet as a seagull
  settling,
And the clocks will stop, and no-one will wonder
  or care or notice,
And people will smile without reason, even in the
  winter,
  even in the rain.

A. S. J. Tessimond, *Daydream*

When I have written this article, and caught up with
the stack of letters waiting to be answered, travelled to
Leeds for this weekend's workshop, waded through
the pile of ironing and when ... soon ... *then* I am very
hopeful that I shall feel free to 'unfold' and 'unfurl' a
little and become less 'knotted up' with activity and
meeting deadlines than I usually am. Or will I? If past
experience is anything to go by such a scenario is
highly unlikely! Yet I persist in deluding myself with
the belief that life will suddenly change and that I shall

find myself with enough time and space to relax into life and enjoy being the serene, organised person God surely meant me to be. I shall 'uncurl'.

Meanwhile I comfort myself with the assumption that it really is not my fault that the luxury of such freedom has escaped me thus far. Pressures and demands have come at me from all sides, circumstances have limited me and, all in all, it is the combination of such extraneous difficulties that now prevent me from viewing life and my participation in it in a more relaxed and constructive way. It is only in my very occasional better moments that I wonder why on earth I so frequently seem incapable of taking to myself one of God's most loving and sustaining gifts – the gift of being able to feel free and at peace whatever one's immediate situation or limitations happen to be.

Of course, 'feeling free' can itself be experienced on many different levels and no doubt, initially, we would all describe what it means to us in differing ways. We might begin from the more superficial understanding of having time to sit and read a novel, or of taking time away from work. We might speak of feeling relieved after a time of particular anxiety or of being released from financial restraint. To relax and feel free in this way is a refreshing and welcome change; we all benefit from such times and should seek to create more of them. But to 'feel free' in its deepest sense is far more crucial to our well-being, and when we allow it to become fundamental to our whole way of life, it is liberating and transcendent and very, very precious.

Those who have known lack of freedom in terms of imprisonment have spoken of the way in which they often focus on particular aspects of freedom. We hear the cry of Joan of Arc in Shaw's play as she is told she will be imprisoned for life:

You promised me my life; but you lied. You
think that life is nothing but not being stone
dead. It is not the bread and water I fear. I can
live on bread: when have I asked for more? It
is no hardship to drink water if water be
clean... But to shut me from the sight of the
fields and flowers; to chain my feet so that I can
never again ride with the soldiers nor climb the
hills; to make me breathe foul damp darkness,
and keep me from everything that brings me
back to the love of God ... all this is worse than
the furnace in the Bible that was heated seven
times. I could do without my warhorse; I could
drag about in a skirt; I could let the banners
and the trumpets and the knights and soldiers
pass me and leave me behind as they leave the
other women, if only I could still hear the wind
in the trees, the larks in the sunshine, the young
lambs crying through the healthy frost, and the
blessed, blessed church bells that send my
angel voices floating to me on the wind. But
without these things I cannot live ...

For Shukov, in Solzhenitsyn's *One Day in the Life of Ivan
Denisovitch*, freedom meant one thing: home – 'But they
wouldn't let him go home.' Yet he found a kind of
freedom in looking for the positive aspects of events
where others would have found nothing good:
'Shukov went to sleep fully content. He'd had many
strokes of luck that day; they hadn't put him in the
cells ... they hadn't sent the team to the settlement –
he'd built a wall and enjoyed doing it . . . he hadn't
fallen ill ... A day without a dark cloud. Almost a
happy day.'

Even when speaking of the bleak horror of Auschwitz,
Ulrich Simon, who lost many of his closest family
there, could say:

The possibility of freedom in slavery is a spiritual act, in which everything that is done is first received.

Thus the freedom of Auschwitz, too, must be wholly distinguished from any system of ethical duties. Its very concreteness derives from the transcendent freedom of the will without which liberation on such a scale cannot be initiated.

Similarly our 'What shall we do?' is still-born even as a question unless it is lifted to the appropriate level of freedom, which is called faith.

For millions of people in the world today – not least the thousands in our own supposedly 'free' country – there is a longing to feel free from all that restricts and imprisons body and soul, to feel free from the hatred engendered by prejudice and discrimination, from the fear of unemployment or homelessness or the effects of poverty, injustice, abuse or neglect. In the perspective of such painful lack of freedom of choice for so many we must never be guilty of talking glibly about the possibility that is meant to be there for all of us to 'feel free' in the way that God intended. And for those of us who possess freedom in a way that others can only dimly imagine there should be no escaping our responsibility to become involved in every personal, social or political way we can, to ensure that every individual is given the greatest possible freedom to live his or her life to the full.

But we are constantly humbled by the knowledge that even in the most constricting and horrendous circumstances countless people still manage to feel free and to live life with courage and humour and satisfaction. And if such inner freedom is possible for them, then with God's help and grace, it is surely on offer for every one of us. In the end it seems that everything can be taken from a person but one thing – the last of the human freedoms – the freedom to choose our attitude in any given set of circumstances. And as Christians we can be left in no doubt that God wants to penetrate our attitudes so that he can free us to enter fully into the heart of life wherever we are and whatever is happening to us.

To feel free in such a way has within it the kingdom quality of becoming like children. It is linked with tenderness and transparency and contentment with the littleness and limitations of life. It is about sensing the wonder in all things, and about looking for the blessing and benediction in relationships, and appreciating the positive possibilities in so much that happens to us. It sees the funny side of ourselves. It cannot flow from being self-centred and it does not bypass reality by taking suffering lightly, but it seeks to perceive the grace and love of God in all things and to be on the side of hope and encouragement and of a simple serenity which is founded on trust.

Yet, paradoxically, to 'feel free' is never an easy option. Rather, it is a costly state of being, in that it necessitates a continual loosening of bonds which constrict us and because, like forgiveness, it has constantly to be born out of self-offering and self-acceptance.

We have to be prepared to 'unfold' and 'unfurl' again and again if we are to 'untie' ourselves sufficiently to recognise the validity of our freedom in quietness of spirit and an overflowing of joy, as Donald Hilton's words convey so magnificently:

Let joy break out, eternal God!
Take the self-imposed blindfold from our eyes,
Rob us of the crutches we so dearly love.
Unshackle mind and heart,
And grant the freedom you have ever planned.
Let joy break out!
Throw open wide the gate to life
And help us find ourselves.

Let joy break out!
And flood our lives;
 creation spilling out its brilliant gifts,
 love finding itself lost in love,
 silence deepened, and all sound enhanced.
Let joy break out! And break again!
 as your fatherly love enfolds us
 as Jesus speaks the intimate Word
 and the Spirit enlivens our half-deadened lives.
Let joy break out! And joy again!

If, with God's loving grace, we learn to 'unshackle our
minds and hearts' in this way we shall know what it is
truly to feel free whatever life has in store for us and all
our petty preoccupation with busyness and pressure
and restrictions will be seen in the light of the loving
freedom which God longs for us to delight in.

I sought for Peace, but could not find;
   I sought it in the city,
But they were of another mind,
   The more's the pity!

I sought for Peace of country swain,
   But yet I could not find;
So I, returning home again,
   Left Peace behind.

Sweet Peace, where dost thou dwell? said I.
   Methought a voice was given:
'Peace dwelt not here, long since did fly
   To God in heaven.'

Thought I, this echo is but vain,
   To folly 'tis of kin;
Anon I heard it tell me plain,
   'Twas killed by sin.

Then I believed the former voice,
   And rested well content,
Laid down and slept, rose, did rejoice,
   And then to heaven went.

There, I enquired for Peace, and found it true,
An heavenly plant it was, and sweetly grew.

                       Samuel Speed

I have often been richly contented in the squalidest garret. One such lodging is often in my memory; it was at Islington not far from the City Road; my window looked down upon the Regent's Canal . . . I recall what was perhaps the worst London fog I ever knew; for three successive days at least my lamp had to be kept burning; when I looked through the window, I saw, at moments, a few blurred lights in the street beyond the canal, but for the most part nothing but a yellowish darkness, which caused the glass to reflect the firelight and my own face. Did I feel miserable? Not a bit of it. The enveloping gloom seemed to make my chimney corner only the more cosy. I had coal, oil, tobacco in sufficient quantity; I had a book to read; I had work which interested me; so I went forth only to get my meals at a City Road coffee shop, and hastened back to the fireside . . . How surprised and indignant I should have felt had I known of anyone who pitied me.

George Gissing, *The Private Papers of Henry Ryecroft*

And I say let a man be of good cheer about his soul. When the soul has been arrayed in her own proper jewels – temperance and justice, and courage, and nobility and truth – she is ready to go on her journey when the hour comes.

Socrates, minutes before his execution

When the truth shines out in the soul, and the soul sees itself in the truth, there is nothing brighter than that light or more impressive than that testimony. And when the splendour of this beauty fills the entire heart it naturally becomes visible, just as a lamp under a bowl or a light in darkness are not there to be hidden. Shining out like rays upon the body, it makes a mirror of itself so that its beauty appears in a man's every action, his speech, his looks, his movements and his smile.

St Bernard

Feeling and the religious mood are eternally the deepest thing of man, the ground of all joy and greatness for him.

Matthew Arnold

Joy has something within itself which is beyond joy and sorrow. This something is called blessedness . . .

This joy which has in itself the depth of blessedness is asked for and promised in the Bible. It preserves itself in its opposite, sorrow. It provides the foundation for happiness and pleasure. It is present in all levels of man's striving for fulfillment. It consecrates and directs them. It does not diminish or weaken them. It does not take away the risks and dangers of the joy of life. It makes the joy of life possible in pleasure and pain, in happiness and unhappiness, in ecstasy and sorrow. Where there is joy, there is fulfillment. And where there is fulfillment, there is joy. In fulfillment and joy the inner aim of life, the meaning of creation, and the end of salvation are attained.

Paul Tillich, *The New Being*

I had been ploughing all day in the black dust of the Lichtenburg roads, and had come very late to a place called the eye of Malmani – Malmani Oog – the spring of a river which presently loses itself in the Kalahari. We watered our horses and went supperless to bed. Next morning I bathed in one of the Malmani pools – and icy cold it was – and then basked in the early sunshine while breakfast was cooking. The water made a pleasant music and nearby was a covert of willows filled with singing birds. Then and there came on me the hour of revelation, when, though savagely hungry, I forgot about breakfast. Scents, sights and sounds blended into a harmony so perfect that it transcended human expression, even human thought. It was like a glimpse of the peace of eternity.

John Buchan, *Memory Hold-the-Door*

The joy that Jesus offers his disciples is his own joy, which flows from his intimate communion with the One who sent him. It is a joy that does not separate happy days from sad days, successful moments from moments of failure, experiences of honour from experiences of dishonour, passion from resurrection. This joy is a divine gift that does not leave us during times of illness, poverty, oppression or persecution. It is present even when the world laughs or tortures, robs or maims, fights or kills. It is truly ecstatic, always moving us away from the house of fear into the house of love, and always proclaiming that death no longer has the final say, though its noise remains loud and its devastation visible. The joy of Jesus lifts up life to be celebrated.

Henri Nouwen, *Life Signs*

Shoulders that Speak

Donald Coggan

It is often possible to tell a good deal about someone's character by the way he holds himself. To put it briefly: *Shoulders can speak.*

Let me explain. Here is a man with shoulders hunched, his muscles taut, his steps hurried. Here is another, shoulders relaxed, muscles loose, head held erect, steps strong and measured. The odds are that, if you looked him in the eye, the first would show a measure of dis-ease, the second a measure of inner rest and calm. A person's serenity – or lack of it – is reflected in his stance.

Serenity? A strange word to bother about, surely, in a world that seems to be going mad largely for lack of people who will rage against wrong, fight against evil, fight and not heed the wounds. I see the point. But stop a minute.

Look at the figure of Jesus. Here was a fighter if ever there was one – he fought our ills of sin, ignorance and disease – fought them to his death on Calvary. Here was no passionless weakling. He could be angry – see him driving out the money-changers from the Temple; see him rebuking Peter – 'Get behind me, *Satan*'; see him denouncing the pity-less and upholding the woman taken in adultery. He could grieve – see him weeping at the grave of Lazarus. If ever there was a man wholly involved in the human plight it was Jesus of Nazareth. He knew what it was to be tired out, to be deserted by his friends and pursued by his foes. His was a ministry of immense and demanding activity.

And yet – the Gospels give us the picture of one who was in charge of things – yes, in charge of himself. One could never describe him as hassled or hectic. Surrounded and hard pressed by the crowds, he is still at peace. He is not rattled. Indeed, on the boat, when the disciples were scared to death by the storm, to their surprise and distress they found him asleep! That picture poses for us the question: *Whence the serenity of Jesus?*

The answer is clear. There was no clash between him and his Father. Their wills were one. 'I do always those things that please him.' In the Father's will was his peace. There was no blockage between them; the power and peace of God could flow into the person of Jesus and out again in a ministry of wholeness. To him there was no other god but his Father-God, and he loved him with all his heart and soul.

Archbishop Stuart Blanch put it well in his little book, *The Ten Commandments*: 'To worship many gods is to live a divided life, drawn this way and that by conflicting desires and conflicting ambitions . . . To worship the one true God is to be on the way to a certain harmony . . . I become one person when I worship one God.' (Hodder and Stoughton 1981, p.32).

'Don't pray to be made gooder but to be made looser and lighter. It's the poets and lovers who get there,' – so wrote Florence Allshorn. Perhaps she had in mind the lines of a poet, Elizabeth Barrett Browning:

> I smiled to think God's greatness flowed round
>   our incompleteness;
> Round our restlessness His rest.

Would it not be true to say that the world's greatest need is an infusion of Christian women and men who are strong enough in God, obedient enough to God, to breathe into the world's hectic hassle something of his peace, and through their silent waiting on God share something of his passion for the world's salvation?

Thus we lived several years in a state of much happiness, not but that we sometimes had those little rubs which Providence sends to enhance the value of its favours. My orchard was often robbed by schoolboys, and my wife's custard plundered by the cats or the children. The Squire would sometimes fall asleep in the most pathetic parts of my sermon, or his lady return my wife's civilities at church with a mutilated courtesy. But we soon got over the uneasiness caused by such accidents, and usually in three or four days began to wonder how they vexed us.

Oliver Goldsmith, *The Vicar of Wakefield*

Very little is needed to make a happy life. It is all within yourself, in your way of thinking.

Marcus Aurelius

You seem to apprehend that I believe religion to be inconsistent with cheerfulness, and with a sociable friendly temper. So far from it, that I am convinced, as true religion or holiness cannot be without cheerfulness, so steady cheerfulness, on the other hand, cannot be without holiness or true religion. And I am equally convinced that religion has nothing sour, austere, unsociable, unfriendly in it; but on the contrary, implies the most winning sweetness, the most amiable softness and gentleness.

John Wesley, 29th March, 1737

SADNESS
&
CONSOLATION

Sorrow is a fruit: God does not make it grow on limbs too weak to bear it.

Victor Hugo

This melancholy second Sunday since my irreparable loss I ventured to church. I hoped it might calm my mind and subject it to its new state – its lost, lost happiness. But I suffered inexpressibly; I sunk on my knees, and could scarcely contain my sorrows, scarcely rise any more! But I prayed – fervently – and I am glad I made the trial, however severe.

Fanny Burney, *Diary*, 17th May, 1818

I hanker too much after a state of happiness, both for myself and others; I cannot face misery with an eye of sufficient firmness; and am little capable of encountering present pain for the sake of any reversionary benefit.

Thomas de Quincey

Why, because there has been a slow decadence of spiritual joy should you come to the conclusion that you are going back instead of forward? You say, 'I have possessed a blessing of inestimable value, but a great dimness has come over it.' Are you measuring your growth by the joy which is but its fruit? But the just shall live by faith. True, the peace of God which passeth all understanding ensures to us joy in the Holy Ghost but it is often a very chastened experience.

Letter in the *Methodist Recorder*, Christmas 1901

Return to Chile

Sheila Cassidy

On Ash Wednesday 1992, I was invited by the BBC to take part in a radio programme entitled 'Unfinished Business'. As the producer explained that participants would be looking back at some significant event in their lives, my heart contracted and I thought, O God! Chile.

I don't know that I'd ever thought about my Chile experience as being unfinished business: after all, I'd studied there, worked for the Church, treated a man on the run, been imprisoned, tortured and expelled as *persona non grata* – surely nothing could be more final than that? It wasn't as if I hadn't explored the psychological aftermath of the experience either: I'd attended conferences on Post Traumatic Stress Disorder, had several years of psychotherapy, done everything I thought I needed to obtain closure on such a pivotal experience – and yet, the moment the issue was raised I knew I had to explore it.

It's hard to convey the degree of ambivalence I felt about the whole affair. I found myself swinging mercilessly between exhilaration and fear – excitement at the idea of revisiting Latin America and a fear of going back that seemed to defy all logic. For a while I let the idea lie dormant but when John Newbury, a Methodist minister from the BBC Religious Affairs Department, telephoned me with the offer that he would accompany me to record the programme I was plunged once more into anguish. The thought of going back made me feel physically sick.

I was afraid of violence, of being abducted, of being tortured, of being killed – but more than anything I was afraid of *fear* itself. It mattered nothing that I knew that my fears were illogical, that Pinochet's dictatorship had been replaced by democracy, the security forces disbanded, the Villa Grimaldi interrogation centre and Tres Alamos prison closed, and that seventeen years had passed since I was put on the plane to England and the British Ambassador recalled in protest at my treatment. In my *head* I knew that the Cassidy Affair was ancient history, but somehow I couldn't get that message through to my guts, and the dragons of my unconscious mind stalked its dark corridors seeking whom they might devour.

Fear is a very tiresome bed fellow and I had been afraid for longer than I liked to admit. In the early days, of course, the night was full of demons. I would lie terrified in my bed listening to the creak of the stair and the rattle of the windows. Each poacher's shot was the military, every dark corner concealed an assassin. I knew even then that it was absurd so I didn't talk about it, but learned to live with my demons, covering my anguish with humour and self mockery.

Fear is not easily banished. It has an animal quality, an existence of its own. It attaches itself like a burr, like a piece of discarded gum to the fabric of one's everyday, to quite ordinary people and events. I am afraid, for example, of crowded pubs – a fear that is so powerful that it will override both hunger and thirst. My heart contracts with terror each time I hear a foreign voice on the telephone – a fear compounded by the fact that the Latins inevitably ring one late in the evening when the defences are down and the heart most vulnerable. It isn't always like that, of course. Most of the time I count myself rich in health and joy, gifted in my work, my friends, my creativity, my faith. But always there is the fear of fear and I travel the world like a neurotic pilgrim, bowed down under the weight of provisions to ward off the terrors of the night: cocoa, whisky, biscuits, a candle to pray by and a bear to hug.

So what would returning to Chile achieve? Would it unlock yet another compartment of Pandora's box, or would it be the spotlight which revealed the box to be empty? I simply did not know. Time and again I had thought the Chile business was over, the cupboard cleared, the discarded clothes bundled off to some psychic jumble sale, the file closed. But little by little, I learned that such files are not easily closed, that they are not necessarily shredded and mercifully incinerated after twenty years but may lie for ever in the pending tray, waiting to be re-opened in error or by design.

My ambivalence about the venture continued unabated and must have made it very difficult for John to plan for the event. Then, in April, something happened which took me totally unawares. Briefly in Dublin, on my way to lecture in Galway, I sought out the Columban Fathers, in whose Santiago house I had been arrested, to see what they would feel about my returning to Chile. I needed to know in particular whether they would be happy to offer John and me hospitality, for I had it at the back of my mind that they would shrink from the idea of publicity and think badly of me for 'exploiting' them and my story. I couldn't, of course, have been more mistaken: they said that it was perfectly safe for me to go back to Chile and that they would be delighted to welcome us both, tape recorders and all, in their Santiago house.

As we drove away from the house in Rahiney I remember saying, 'Well, that settles it. Now there's nothing to stop me going back.' How dense I must have been to have missed, even for a moment, the connection between that event and the torment which followed so quickly in its wake.

Pathological Anxiety is a singularly nasty form of fear, common enough but, absurdly, not often talked about. How could I, as a doctor, have been so ignorant of it, I wonder? How could I fail to connect the appalling giddiness I experienced during that train ride from Dublin to Galway with the conversation with the Columbans less than two hours before? What in God's name did I think was happening to me as I sat there glued to my seat thinking, 'I'm going to have a stroke. I'm going to die. Something terrible has befallen me.'

As the days went by the physical manifestations of my anxiety state came and went. I delivered lectures, attended dinners, went for car drives and hoped it would all go away – but it didn't. When eventually I sought medical help I was spiralling down into a depressive illness, unable to sleep and wrestling in the early hours with suicidal fantasies. The treatment of that illness, the support I received, is another story. Suffice to say that I entered into a period of intensive psychotherapy to prepare myself for the Chile trip. Whatever it was we did in those sessions, the psychiatrist and I, as I faced my fears again and again, wept over them, drew them, described them, seems to have worked, for eventually I found myself on the plane to Miami and then *en route* to Santiago.

Now, it is over and I sit knitting in the Florida sunshine, thankful that I had the sense to build this time of reflection into my schedule, that I had the foresight to know that there would be things to be processed, memories to be savoured, and that it would be foolhardy to return immediately to work with its multiplicity of demands, its incomprehension of the contemplative.

I went to tea, yesterday, with some enclosed sisters and, as they bade me tell how the visit to Chile had been, I found myself cringing, not yet ready to articulate to these kind women what they wanted to hear – that I believed that I had somehow been healed of the pain of the past seventeen years, that the dragons of my fear had been slain. One of them asked if I had met the people who had held me captive – and I shrank even further into my chair muttering that no, I hadn't, and that I wouldn't have recognised them anyway because I had always been blindfold in their presence.

I did tell them, however, of the amazing kindness of my Columban hosts and of the support I had received from John Newbury during the making of our programme – but I could not yet speak of the fear that possessed me as I stood outside Tres Alamos (for many years a prison for political detainees) and heard the friend who was with me mention my name to the guard to try to persuade him to let us in. Tres Alamos, it seems, is still a place of detention. It would have been absurd, I suppose, to waste those high walls with their barbed wire on some ordinary enterprise, like a school or a factory. I wonder whether the present inmates (young delinquents) have any inkling of their prison's former use, whether they sense the presence of those passionate young women, now old enough to be their mothers. Surely Sabrina at least must have left some spoor – arrested in her school uniform – at seventeen years already a prison veteran having spent time in the stadium after the coup.

I found Tres Alamos scary and wanted to get out, sure that the guard must already be on the 'phone to some higher authority to say that I was back and was causing trouble.

I looked at Jane and Liz, the two sisters who had accompanied us and felt a profound respect for their quiet endurance during all those years of dictatorship. It was only now that I learned that each time they came to visit me in prison they had queued for two hours and then been strip-searched. How they managed to smuggle the consecrated host into the prison, Lord only knows. We went on from Tres Alamos to the Villa Grimaldi. There had been those who said there was no point in even looking for the Grimaldi, that it had been demolished, built over, changed beyond recognition. But they were wrong. That infamous house of torture, where so many men and women were stripped naked and interrogated, where the strong elite among the revolutionaries were confined in cages, is very much in existence. It stands where it has always stood, in the Calle Jose Arieta, in the area known as Penalolen, tucked under the shadow of the warm brown hills of the Cordillera. True, the buildings inside have been demolished but the high red adobe walls with their heavy iron gates, which I and so many others heard slam behind them, are there for anyone to see.

Astonishingly, (for I still find it difficult to believe that the security forces no longer care what is said about them) the walls of the Grimaldi are covered with murals. The Chileans have a rich tradition of political graffiti and the paintings we saw were unbelievably poignant. The message, 'These walls cannot hide torture and assassination' was immaculately inscribed in artists' letters, as were other less inflammatory words such as, 'La Justicia solo vive cuando la injusticia muere' – Justice can only live when injustice dies. Perhaps the very fact that the Grimaldi paintings are there for anyone to see, even to film, is a sign that justice is beginning once again to take hold in Chile.

One of the most moving drawings was a *pietà* composition in which a desolate figure cries out to heaven while supporting on his or her lap a lifeless body. On another wall was a drawing of a group of prisoners in chains, among them a woman great with child. The woman and her foetus were portrayed in a line drawing, a powerful reminder that even advanced pregnancy neither safeguarded women prisoners nor earned them respect from their captors. I remember so well the cry of my fellow prisoners – 'They did not respect me as a woman.' I remember, too, the terrible story of one New Year's Eve in which the guards at the Grimaldi got drunk and raped all the women in their charge. There was trouble later of course, for such behaviour constitutes a serious breach of security.

The future of the Grimaldi lies in the balance right now: it had been bought for a housing development but the protest was such that the government have put a temporary embargo upon the sale whilst they consider the popular demand that it should be preserved as a place of remembrance, a park of peace.

On the Saturday afternoon of my visit I was entertained to lunch by some of my 'classmates' – my fellow gaolbirds from Tres Alamos prison. There were eleven of them: the lovely Anita Maria who gave me her hair clip the day I was moved from solitary confinement to Tres Alamos, Gladys Diaz, the intelligent, stalwart journalist who had been the only prisoner to have survived incarceration in the cages, and many more. For my missionary friend Jane there was a joyous reunion with Sabrina whom she had hidden in her poblacion convent.

We all knew, of course, at that riotous lunch party, how lucky we were to be there – lucky not to have been *disappeared* like so many other prisoners. You didn't have to be particularly important to vanish: sometimes there seemed no reason. There was one foolish lady, mother of an actress, who found a piece of left wing propaganda lying in the street. Thinking it might cheer her daughter up she took it with her on visiting day and was arrested when her bag was searched. The last time she was seen was during that infamous New Year in the Grimaldi. The girls said she couldn't really understand what was happening because she'd always thought of herself as a supporter of the military government.

It was a great re-union. We ate steak and salad and drank wine with strawberries, and sang old songs: 'Venceremos', the song of Allende's revolution, a Spanish version of Beethoven's 'Ode to Joy' and an old favourite, 'Animo, Negro Jose' ('Take heart, Joe my love'). The last time we'd all sung that, I think, was Christmas night of 1975 when we stood on chairs in the prison yard bursting our lungs in order to reach the five hundred men prisoners the other side of the wall.

I never really caught up with the words of 'Animo, Negro Jose' but I took a childish pleasure in being the first to recall the lines of 'Venceremos' ('We Shall Overcome'):

> From the deep crucible of our country
> there arises the cry of the people;
> the new dawn is announced,
> all Chile begins to sing.

But, of course, not all Chile wanted to sing that particular song, not everyone was happy to break the 'thousand chains' that held its poor captive. The revolutionaries thought they had the answer to the sub-human living of so many of its families – but history was to decree otherwise.

So what of Chile now? What is it like now that dictatorship has given way to democracy? Everyone I met asked me how I found the country, whether I thought it greatly changed. It's difficult to give this question the measured answer it deserves, better perhaps to quote some of my friends who live there now. Democracy, it seems, has rooted well and is flourishing under the prudent governance of Patricio Alwyn. Everyone I spoke to seemed happy to move slowly rather than risk any kind of destabilisation. Friends who should know told me that the poor are not quite as poor as in years gone by – there are fewer hungry, fewer barefoot children in the poblaciones. The gulf, however, between rich and poor is greater than it has been despite Chile's economic boom. The Barrio Alto, the upper-class region of the town, is full of new developments, shops, apartment blocks, a luxury Hyatt Hotel. The people I saw in this part of town were superbly dressed with that wonderful Latin American elegance that can make a Parisienne look dowdy.

In other parts of the town, at the far end of Santiago's shining new metro, I saw many beggars. There were pale faced women trying to sell lace and a woman slumped on the subway steps, unmoving beside her tin cup placed ready for the odd coin. I went several times to the poblaciones, twice to visit my former housekeeper, and a couple of times to the houses of the missionaries. The people I saw in the street inhabit a very different world to the beautiful people of the

Barrio Alto, but the children I saw were lively and the streets were full of lovers and men and women happily going about their business. Clearly there is structural injustice, but of overt repression I saw no sign.

On November 25th John and I left Santiago, laden with presents and souvenirs from a craft fair. Just before we left for the airport, we celebrated a mass of thanksgiving for the visit. It's a long time since I have felt so fully part of a eucharistic liturgy. There were four or five of the Columban fathers, Mercedes my housekeeper, sisters Jane and Liz, two Peruvian ladies and, briefly, the house pet, a white rabbit called *Resu* (for resurrection). That absurd Easter Bunny had been my delight during these magic days of cherishing in the Columban centre home, a symbol of freedom and vulnerability with which I identified so powerfully. It mattered nothing that this was the house where I'd been arrested, that the bullet marks are still clearly in evidence on the wall, the floor and ancient fridge. I can recall without undue pain that night when I was detained and interrogated. I have revisited the place of my torture, and I have written to President Alwyn supporting the move that the Grimaldi be preserved as a park of peace.

I have come away with a handful of dusty flowers from outside the prison – but, more important, with peace in my heart. Whether it has been the confrontation of my fears or the tender care of friends, the reunion with fellow prisoners or the love of a white rabbit, I shall probably never sort out. But this I know – that I am glad that I found courage to return and grateful to all who supported me. I have done what I set out to do: to reclaim for myself the freedom to walk alone and unafraid in a city that I love.

Then first I knew the delight of being lowly; of saying to myself, 'I am what I am, nothing more.' 'I have failed,' I said, 'I have lost myself – would it had been my shadow.' I looked round: the shadow was nowhere to be seen. Ere long, I learned that it was not myself, but only my shadow, that I had lost. I learned that it is better, a thousand-fold, for a proud man to fall and be humbled, than to hold up his head in his pride and fancied innocence. I learned that he that will be a hero, will barely be a man; that he that will be nothing but a doer of his work, is sure of his manhood.

George Macdonald, *Phantastes*

It is not to die, or even to die of hunger, that makes a man wretched ... But it is to live miserable; to be heart worn, weary, yet isolated, unrelated, girt-in with a cold universal 'laissez faire'. This is, and remains, forever intolerable to all men whom God has made.

Thomas Carlyle, Past and Present

I am already beginning to forget the house and it is only occasionally when reading or writing, that I suddenly and quite unexpectedly remember the green light of the window and the sound of my footsteps echoing in the fields at night as I returned home, full of my love, and rubbed my hands because of the cold. Even more rarely, at times when I am sad and weary with loneliness, I have indistinct memories, and gradually begin to feel that I too am remembered, that I am expected and that we shall meet ... My darling, where are you?

Anton Chekhov

There is a story in the Talmud of a man who had a little daughter. She was his only child and when she became sick and died the father was filled with grief. His friends tried to comfort him, but he would not be comforted. Then one night he had a dream. He seemed to be in heaven and many little girls were there, acting their parts in a pageant. Each one carried a lighted candle, except for one whose candle was not lit. Looking more closely, he saw that the child with the unlit candle was his daughter. He took her in his arms and caressed her, then asked her why her candle was not burning like the others. 'Often it does light,' she answered him, 'but your tears keep making it go out.'

Mystery and miracle once meant the same thing. Now, as we orient ourselves to a new way of living, those two words may have again the same meaning. There are many things that cannot be explained. To try to force an explanation in pursuit of the mystery may, in this case, lessen the miracle. Don't try to grapple with the event of death with logic, but meet it with faith.

Elizabeth Yates, *Up the Golden Stair*

Lord, we pray for those who know intense suffering:
for those who groan with hunger
for those whose bodies are racked with pain through illness
for those who ache with loneliness
for those whose bodies are tired out with hard work
for those whose spirits are numbed by constant denial of their
    humanity
for those whose will is exhausted through failure
for those who know crushing sorrow.

Lord, you have the clear, sparkling water of life within you;
and you share humanity's experience of shed blood; we pray
for all who suffer, that they may know your solidarity in the
intensity of their pain, and also receive the advocacy of the
Holy Spirit to comfort and uplift them. Help them to find a
faith that protects their inmost self from destruction; to
experience the love and peace of God which no suffering can
shut out if our faith keeps us open to you: to find an
assurance of spiritual life which is renewed in vigour each
day. We also pray that in our human mortality they may find
hope of salvation as it is received in bread, healing,
companionship, rest for body and mind, affirmation for the
person they are, real achievement and meaningful goals, and
joy, fresh each morning. And for those who will not find
relief in this life we pray that you will impart courage and
faith that their life was not lived in vain. Through Jesus
Christ our Lord. Amen.

Denis Vernon

83

When Jesus came to Golgotha they hanged him on a
  tree,
They drove great nails through hands and feet and
  made a Calvary;
They crowned him with a crown of thorns; red were
  his wounds, and deep,
For those were crude and cruel days, and human
  flesh was cheap.

When Jesus came to Birmingham they simply passed
  him by,
They never hurt a hair of him, they only let him die;
For men had grown more tender, and they would
  not give him pain,
They only just passed down the street, and left him
  in the rain.

Still Jesus cried, 'Forgive them, for they know not
  what they do,'
And still it rained a wintry rain that drenched him
  through and through;
The crowds went home and left the streets without a
  soul to see,
And Jesus crouched against a wall and cried for
  Calvary.

G. A. Studdert Kennedy

Ash Wednesday in Nazareth

Pauline Warner

Mary brushed her hand against her cheek to wipe away the tear. Joseph got up from his seat next to the fire and came to stand at his wife's side. With no words having been spoken, he still knew exactly what she was thinking. Tenderly, his hand followed the same path as her own and wiped away the trail of flour. Her cheek was just as pale as before.

'Let him go.' His voice was gentle but firm. 'We knew it was to come to this. You have done your task. Now he must begin his own work. We always knew he would be ours for just a time.'

'But have I done enough?'

There was no impatience but only confidence in Joseph's quick reply. 'You will never know how much you have done for him. Now no more tears. Too much salt spoils the flavour of bread!'

Mary laughed inwardly and that laugh showed in her eyes. As always he was right. The old man returned to resume his seat. 'Please take this and put it in the hearth,' she asked, 'It's ready for proving.'

As his frail old fingers lifted up the bowl, Mary remembered a time when it was a young boy's strengthening hands processing that same dish. She remembered a day when he had asked, 'Why?' and they had sat together by the fire and she had tried to find the childlike words to explain that, when the dough has been well prepared, it needs to stand in a place of warmth so that the yeast can begin to fill it through and through and make it grow. 'Why does it need to grow?' he had asked, and Mary had wondered where do children learn the question, 'Why?' but she needed no answer this time. For he had added with that knowing seriousness which only five-year-olds possess, 'I suppose it's so there will be more for us to eat.'

They certainly needed plenty of bread nowadays. The places at their table had long been filled with their growing family of sons and daughters and now grandchildren. Yet as Mary started to set out the plates and dishes, she felt keenly that there would be an empty place this evening. But Joseph was right. No more tears. She had done her task and perhaps some things that she had said and done would help him about his Father's business.

And somewhere, many miles away, her eldest son knelt. He had to be apart for a time in this place of desert heat that his Father's will might come to fill every fibre of his being. Before he gave himself to be broken for the feeding of the whole world.

Jesus, Bread of Life
who was prepared
in a mother's kitchen as well as a Father's Temple
knead us into shape this Lent
that we may truly rise with you on Easter Day.

The day is cold, and dark, and dreary;
It rains; and the wind is never weary;
The vine still clings to the mouldering wall,
But at every gust the dead leaves fall,
    And the day is dark and dreary.

My life is cold, and dark, and dreary;
It rains, and the wind is never weary;
My thoughts still cling to the mouldering Past
But the hopes of youth fall thick in the blast,
    And the days are dark and dreary.

Be still, sad heart! and cease repining;
Behind the clouds is the sun still shining;
Thy fate is the common fate of all;
Into each life some rain must fall;
    Some days must be dark and dreary.

                    Henry Wadsworth Longfellow

We feel at first as if some opportunities of kindness and sympathy were lost, but learn afterwards that any pure grief is ample recompense for all. That is, if we are faithful; for a spent grief is but sympathy with the soul that disposes events, and is as natural as the resin of Arabian trees. Only nature has a right to grieve perpetually, for she only is innocent. Soon the ice will melt and the blackbirds sing along the river which he frequented, as pleasantly as ever. The same everlasting serenity will appear in this face of God, and we will not be sorrowful, if he is not.

H. D. Thoreau

'Oliver!' said Mr Bumble.

'Yes, sir,' replied Oliver, in a low, tremulous voice.

'Pull that cap off your eyes, and hold up your head, sir.'

Although Oliver did as he was desired, at once; and passed the back of his unoccupied hand briskly across his eyes, he left a tear in them when he looked up at his conductor. As Mr Bumble gazed sternly upon him, it rolled down his cheek. It was followed by another, and another. The child made a strong effort, but it was an unsuccessful one. Withdrawing his other hand from Mr Bumble's, he covered his face with both; and wept until the tears sprung out from between his thin and bony fingers.

Charles Dickens, *Oliver Twist*

Joy and sorrow are sisters surely, and very like each other too, or else both would not bring tears as they do equally.

J. R. Lowell

Four things come not back – the spoken word, the sped arrow, the past life and the neglected opportunity.

Arabian proverb

Mr Harding was a sadder man than he had ever yet been when he returned to his own house. He had been wretched enough . . . when he was forced to expose before his son-in-law the publisher's account for ushering into the world his dear book of sacred music; when after making such payments as he could do unassisted, he found he was a debtor of more than three hundred pounds; but his sufferings then were as nothing to his present misery – then he had done wrong and he knew it, and was able to resolve that he could not sin in like manner again; but now he could make no resolution, and comfort himself by no promises of firmness. He had been forced to think that his lot had placed him in a false position, and he was about to maintain that position against the opinion of the world and against his own convictions.

Anthony Trollope, *The Warden*

The day I stopped by to visit one of our church members, I discovered that she was having a very difficult time. Her life was filled with one tragedy after another. She told me that sometimes she woke up in the morning not knowing how she was going to face the day as she wondered what sort of tragedy would come next. But then the tension in the muscles of her face seemed to relax, her mouth began to form a smile, her eyes began to brighten, and she said, 'You know what I do? Every night I sit down with my Bible; I start to read and pray, and during those times it is as if Jesus is so close I could reach out and touch him. That is what gets me through.' That is exactly what Jesus promised. He gives us himself; we are never left alone.

James A. Harnish, *Jesus Makes the Difference!*

I never knew what sad work the reading of old letters was before that evening, though I could hardly tell why. The letters were as happy as letters could be – at least those early letters were. There was in them a vivid and intense sense of the present time, which seemed so strong and full, as if it could never pass away, and as if the warm, living hearts that so expressed themselves could never die and be as nothing to the sunny earth. I should have felt less melancholy, I believe, if the letters had been more so. I saw the tears stealing down the well-worn furrows of Miss Mattie's cheeks, and her spectacles often wanted wiping.

Elizabeth Gaskell, *Cranford*

Let nothing disturb thee,
Nothing affright thee;
All things are passing:
God never changeth;
Patient endurance
Attaineth to all things;
Who God possesseth
In nothing is wanting;
Alone God sufficeth.

St Teresa

He lays no great burden upon us; a little remembrance of him from time to time; a little adoration; sometimes to pray for his grace, sometimes to offer him your sorrows, and sometimes to offer him thanks for the benefits he has given you, and still gives you, in the midst of your troubles. He asks you to console yourself with him the oftenest you can. Lift up your heart to him even at your meals when you are in company; the least little remembrance will always be acceptable to him. You need not cry very loud; he is nearer than you think.

Brother Lawrence

Discovery in Prayer

I exclaimed, 'Hallelujah!' The word came as a surprise, not only to the consultant neurologist who had just informed me that I had a tumour on my spine but to me also. But it *was* said in exultation. For several weeks I had limped about, wondering if I had an untreatable disease. Now this diagnosis at last made sense of the deteriorating condition that I had been experiencing over the previous months. Not only that, but from that moment to the present, some six months later, when I am back at work at least part time, I have been mightily aware of an overriding assurance that all would be well.

I have tried to analyse these experiences both in Addenbrooke's, where I went for surgery, and in the days of convalescence that followed, and I want to pay tribute to a whole army of people, many of whom I shall never know, who wrought the miracle of healing as much with their prayers as did the surgeon with his knowledge and skill.

Let me try to explain this assurance. I had in the past preached on many occasions about the efficacy of prayer. My words then were born of faith, but now I want to assert that I speak from real knowledge. It wasn't an assurance that I would be *cured* in the way that we normally use that word, but it was that, whatever happened – and I was aware that there were dreadful risks involved in the surgery – the outcome could only be good. Perhaps it is not out of place to make the distinction between the words *healed* and *cured*. So often we pray to be healed, but what we are really asking for is to be cured of whatever particular

92

malady ails us at that time. I believe that healing is far more important, for what we are in fact praying for is to be made whole; and surely that is the goal of every Christian.

But there is a sense in which it was more than assurance: it was an abandonment experience (some call it detachment). Only recently I came across these anonymous words:

> What is an abandonment experience? Is it leaving oneself on God's doorstep, walking into the rest of life not allowing anxiety, fear, frustration to enter into one? Is it expecting God to keep one warm, secure and safe, unharmed? Is that abandonment? Abandonment is nothing to do with warmth of womb or arms or clothes or clasped hands. It is not something done by a child. It is done to him or her. It cannot be done to an adult. It is done by him or her. Abandonment is committed only with and in the maturity of Jesus Christ. It is not just a hanging loose. It is a letting go. It is a severing of the things by which one manipulates, controls, administers the forces in one's life. Abandonment is receiving all things the way one receives a gift, with open hands, and opened heart. Abandonment to God is the climactic point in anyone's life.

As a result of the pastoral care and prayers of so many people, I found myself in this state of abandonment. Probably for the first time in my life – although of course I should have known earlier – I realised that I had nothing to give my Lord. I remembered with shame all the times I had prayed for those things that I thought I needed to fulfil me as a person. Now all that

I had to offer was my own poverty, and my Lord took that poverty from my empty hands and returned riches beyond belief. The feeling was so all-encompassing that I can honestly say that, from the moment of diagnosis until now, it felt totally wrong to pray for my own condition. What hurt were the effects that condition was having on those dear to me, and they were the subject of my own prayer life.

So the next time you are asked to pray for someone, please do it. I do not pretend to understand fully how the power of love is summoned up by individuals in this way, but I do assert with every fibre of my being that it works and goes on working.

Waste no tears over the griefs of yesterday.

Euripides

You will break the bow if you always keep it bent.

Greek proverb

The gem cannot be polished without friction, nor man perfected without trials.

Confucius

To one of his spiritual children our dear father (St Francois de Sales) said, 'Be patient with everyone, but above all with yourself. I mean, do not be disheartened by your imperfections, but always rise up with fresh courage. I am glad you make a fresh beginning daily; there is no better means of attaining to the spiritual life than by continually beginning again, and never thinking that we have done enough. How are we to be patient in bearing with our neighbour's faults, if we are impatient in bearing with our own? He who is fretted by his own failings will not correct them; all profitable correction comes from a calm, peaceful mind.'

Jean Pierre Camus

With the sun hanging low on its western limit, the expanse of the grasslands framed in the counter scarps of the rising ground took on a gorgeous and sombre aspect. A sense of penetrating sadness, like that inspired by a grave strain of music, disengaged itself from the silence of the fields. The men we met walked past, slow, unsmiling, with downcast eyes, as if the melancholy of an overburdened earth had weighted their feet, bowed their shoulders, borne down their glances.

Joseph Conrad, *Amy Foster*

Behind joy and laughter there may be a temperament, coarse, hard and callous. But behind sorrow there is always sorrow. Pain, unlike pleasure, wears no mask.

Oscar Wilde, *De Profundis*

I met between thirty and forty colliers and their wives and administered the sacrament to them; but found no comfort myself in that or in any ordinance. I always find strength for the work of the ministry; but when my work is over, my strength, both bodily and spiritually, leaves me. I can pray for others but not for myself. God by me strengthens the weak hands, and confirms the feeble knees; yet am I myself as a man in whom is no strength. I am weary and faint in mind, longing continually to be discharged.

Charles Wesley, 16th September, 1739

Losing a Partner

Maureen Newcombe

Facing life alone is a situation in which one half of every couple find themselves at some time – quite a staggering fact.

Normally when we talk of facing life alone, we think of the separation brought about by the death of one partner. Painful and shattering though that is, it is a sad fact of today's society that marriage breakdowns are on the increase, and I believe we have a responsibility not to forget the pain and distress often experienced in loss by divorce. Are we not guilty of sometimes shrugging it off with a 'Well, that's life.' As one who has experienced both types of bereavement, believe me, this latter situation is also a very lonely and distressing experience. When a husband or wife announces to their partner that, as far as they are concerned, their marriage is at an end, it is devastating.

I loved my husband dearly. We had two lovely daughters and I felt we were a real family unit. But happen to me it did, and I had to face up to it and cope with it. Times of examination followed – Where did it all go wrong? – and when? – followed by the feelings of failure and, yes, bitterness at being cast aside for someone else, as was my case. What about those marriage vows made so solemnly?

It isn't just a private and personal failure, it has to be announced to family and friends. In my case, because my parents were of the 'old school', I just could not bring myself to talk to my mother about the inevitable break up of our twenty-three years of marriage. When I did she was marvellous and I wished I had gone to her much earlier.

I most certainly did not give up without a fight, but I lost the battle. It is humiliating and hurtful to have to tell your friends, but real friends are *very* real at times like this. I have to admit, though, that my faith took a bit of a beating at that time. I felt as if the world around me had collapsed. Nothing made sense. I was wobbling and searching for firm ground. I had to give up my cherished local preaching. I was empty, with nothing to offer any more. I couldn't even find words for my prayers, I was desperately reaching to receive, just hanging on, hoping for a miracle. I didn't even feel the 'church' was very sympathetic or supportive, but I wondered how they could be, when circumstances had forced me to break the rules!

My husband did not move out completely, and he continued to support us financially until the house was sold. How I hated seeing the 'For Sale' board in the garden of the house and home we had built up together, and I felt like shouting 'Listen to my cry for I am in desperate need.' (Psalm 142:6.)

The house market was very slow and it took many months to sell, making the whole awful business very protracted, so when the actual break came some time later, I had had some considerable time to get used to it. But it was still as painful as at the first moment. I really felt at the bottom of the barrel.

There is nothing easy about losing your partner this way – many things take a knock. Self-confidence disappears down the drain. My family and friends tried to help me, and of course life went on. My elder daughter had by this time left home to begin her nursing training. Of necessity I had to have a full time job, and my younger daughter and I moved into a small but comfortable house; but she had always seen nothing but sunshine in her dad, and could not adapt to life without him. Within six months she, too, had left home and moved two hundred miles away. Three months later my mother died, and I even felt my situation had contributed to her death.

Financially it was a real struggle and several of the luxuries of life had to go, including the car. I was back to my bicycle again. That in itself was a blessing. I was able to see again the beauty around me, and brake quickly to chat to a neighbour. With no television I listened to the radio again, and that made me much more aware of its importance to those who just cannot see. Although these days were very hard I now realise they taught me much and added a certain richness to my life. We have to work our way through many things when faced with marriage breakdown.

I am in no way proud to admit that my church attendance was not at all regular. I felt I had let myself and all that I held dear down completely. Of course divorce is against Christian teaching and so often it is the case that the church family does not open its arms very widely to this kind of situation. I pay special tribute to my minister at that time who was a great support and in his loving and quiet way just would not let me fall down completely. I coped with the hostile and distant folk, persuading myself that they had no idea of the pain and anguish so how could they possibly understand, and the prayers and help received from all the others more than made up for their lack of compassion.

A new church had been built and my minister, in his kindly wisdom, was sure 'I was right' for one or two of the committees. Life began gradually to come together again and I began gradually to recognise God's supporting and guiding hand in my life. I entered into new experiences and took on fresh commitments. After a number of years of emptiness, my life suddenly took on a whole new meaning when I met and married Don. We enjoyed every minute. He encouraged me back into the pulpit again. We laughed, we prepared and we prayed together. We wondered –

> Why hast thou cast our lot
> In the same age and place,
> And why together brought
> To see each other's face . . ?

– but we thanked God that he had . . . Then, bang, I was alone again. No time even to say goodbye.

Losing a partner by death is different, it seems so final. No matter how much warning you may have had, the knowledge that your loved one has died is a shock. I had but the shortest of warnings. I was shattered, and for a short while words failed to express just how I felt. The blow came quite suddenly, after a full and active life truly spent in working and caring for others. Don was fifty-nine, I was fifty-two, and we had been given less than five years together.

As someone else has said, 'Suddenly the wheel of my life stopped again, stillness replaced action, and the sounds of life disappeared into silence.'

How do you come to terms with it all? All experiences and reactions are different. Again I can only write from my own experience. To most I seemed to be 'coping very well'. Inside, I was sore, so incomplete, as if part of me had gone too. I went through the usual feelings of disbelief to acceptance that it really had happened to me. At times I wanted to close myself off, shut everyone out, and allow no one to look in. This must have been puzzling and maybe hurtful to my family and friends who were there all over again. As my family had grown there were now more of them, more friends too, but out of loving kindness they almost smothered me. I loved them all. I appreciated all they were trying to do. There were many beds for me to sleep in, many shoulders to cry on, but what was most difficult for them to understand was that I wanted *my* bed, I wanted to cry alone. 'I know how you feel,' they said – I wanted to scream 'How *can* you know?' 'Time is a great healer,' they said – I wanted to scream 'How do you know?' 'Why did it have to happen to someone like him?' they said – I wanted to scream 'Don't ask.' But, of course, I didn't.

Oh yes, I questioned. I couldn't understand, I had no answers – my husband and best friend had gone. He was a great man, an unselfish man, and we had wanted to do so much together. In retrospect I thank God for all the support I received. I was being carried along on a cushion of love and prayer and after a while smiled through the tears as I came to the conclusion that the best tribute I could pay Don would be to carry on loving life, as he most certainly did, and to try to continue with the various work and services we had enjoyed doing together so much. It was desperately hard at times but I am convinced it was the right thing to do, and at times he has been so near as I have moved forward from that time.

I cried. There is no shame in tears. We must grieve *our* way, and our ways can differ very much indeed. When the mother of a friend of mine died, her father didn't even mention her name for over a year, and this upset my friend very much, she just couldn't understand why. It just couldn't be a case of out of sight out of mind. Later her father told her he just could not talk about his wife, it hurt him too much. He grieved inside and as soon as he felt able to he explained to his family. Another friend of mine became very worried because her father insisted on going to his late wife's grave every day, for a quiet time, for weeks. That was his way of working through his grief.

We all have our own particular way. For me, when the initial numbness had worn off, I wanted to talk my way through it, and how surprising it is to see obvious embarrassment in some people when you begin to talk about the one who has died. But again, thankfully, I had family and friends who would just let me 'go on', listening to me, appreciating my need. I do firmly believe we should be allowed to grieve in our own particular way, without too much advice about the things we ought and ought not to do.

Maybe life is sometimes a bit cruel. For me more years together would have been lovely. All who enjoy a happy partnership could say that, however long or short they are together. I treasure the years we had together, and thank God for them. Don was very special.

The soul is in heaven, but memories are on earth. If it helps, bring out the photographs, bring out the paper cuttings. Memories are precious and they are ours. Relive that day on the beach, or the time he dressed up as Father Christmas, laugh again at the hat made for the Easter Bonnet Parade. It's good to talk over old times – all times are part of our rich pattern of life. As some depart, others are added, and I find my grandchildren are interested and enjoy the stories of the past.

Both experiences of losing my partner were heartbreaking, but whereas the divorce shot a few bullet holes in my faith quite the reverse happened with my second loss. Once I had recovered from the obvious shock I realised that had Don lived through the heart attack he would have had to cope with restrictions probably beyond his limitations of acceptance and maybe mine too. He was spared all this, and because I knew him so well and loved him so much I can only be thankful.

Some things will always be difficult. I miss his supporting presence in many things, not least when I am leading worship, because he was always with me. At other times the little remark, favourite hymn or piece of music, or any other unexpected reminder, jerks the tears. Walking into the empty house was difficult for some time. No one to discuss things with after a good (or bad as the case may be) church meeting, evening with a friend, day out; no one with whom to discuss the issues of the day, no one to share and understand your innermost thoughts and concerns. The house is just too quiet. Yet inside your own home, you can be really you, and hopefully find an inner peace.

> The Lord said, 'My grace is all you need, for my power is greatest when you are weak'.
>
> 2 Corinthians 12:9

Making yourself do things and go places alone can be most difficult, for, daft though it may seem, you can feel desperately lonely in a crowd. Yet we all know we must go on. I well remember the tears springing to my eyes when I overheard a conversation between a couple, who were complete strangers to me, in the clothes department of a well known store. She said to him, 'Only your best friend would be completely honest about that tie,' and he said, 'Well, tell me then, you are not only my wife but my best friend too.' And I immediately thought – it's just not fair. I dare say we all creep away into a corner with damp eyes occasionally, perhaps don't even make it to the corner, but it doesn't matter. Thank God for those near to us who just love us through.

Well, I'm glad I didn't scream . . . time does dim the pain.

> Days of darkness still come o'er me,
> Sorrow's path I often tread,
> But the Saviour still is with me,
> By His hand I'm safely led.

> F. H. Rowley

At first, when you lose your partner, in either circumstances, though much more so when it is by death, you are surrounded: lovely folk visit or telephone, flowers arrive and letters and cards tumble through your letterbox, but quite quickly it all stops, of course, and that is a very lonely time. Other crises and problems arise in other people's lives, needing time and attention, and the friends who were your help and lifeline have gone on to help others – and we would have it no other way. But, first, anniversaries have to be faced, wedding, birthdays – theirs and yours – Christmas, and the anniversary of the death, and they are extremely painful. In my case my family and close friends were very sensitive and caring, but then it comes to the second year and, yes, it's not so bad, but on such days it still hurts, and quite naturally, other folk don't remember.

I have passed through two quite similar tunnels, but there was a light at the end of them both; how glad I am I didn't quite lose sight of this, and every day took me nearer to it.

The Psalmist says 'My times are in your hands' and life's journey is one of faith. 'Be strong and of good courage.'

It is mighty hard at times, but then we were never promised it would be easy, and through all things *nothing* shall separate us from the love of God.

We, who have known loss, have so much to give. It is not the end, it could be a new beginning. It is a needy world, and this is one area in which we can truly minister for God in a very special way. *We have been there* and with God's help we can walk alongside the bereaved – not at a distance – and listen for hours on end to the hurt half of a broken marriage. The words of our conversations and prayers can be so much more meaningful.

We may have had to pay dearly – but how rich we are. A wealth to share, to make our future one of true compassion, real encouragement and rich blessing.

On we go – what a mission – and it is ours.

Five years on – Retired, removed, remarried

I went on building using to the best of my ability good healthy bricks of friendship, concern and care; and when I had the opportunity of training as a CRUSE

Bereavement Counsellor I felt it was absolutely right for me to do so, as I had written five years earlier – *I had been there* and felt I could walk alongside. During the last three or four years my life has been greatly enriched by those I have tried to help through all kinds of stages of their bereavement. My new life pattern was shaping up nicely. Retirement loomed, when I knew I would lose the close contact of valued work colleagues, and so another chapter was about to begin.

It has begun – but it is so different to expectations. A fellowship weekend for local preachers and their partners provided an opportunity for conversation with a number still fighting the battle of loneliness. One of the company whom I was endeavouring to encourage was of such a giving and caring nature himself we were soon chatting easily. Letters followed the weekend and then telephone calls and we both found ourselves looking forward to hearing from the other.

Several months later another weekend brought us together again, and we knew beyond any shadow of doubt we wanted to spend what years remained for us together. We both had so much to give to each other and to those around us. We were separated by one hundred and seventy miles. Alan was already retired and so, undaunted, did most of the travelling. Two weeks after I retired we married, and after much prayerful thought I moved to join Alan, and we are happily serving God in the beautiful Cheshire countryside. We thank God daily for this new life, which is so very good. Each day is precious – our blessings are countless.

TRUST
&
RECONCILIATION

*There is great reason that we should
trust the Invisible God farther
than we can see him.*

*John Wesley,
9th February, 1782*

It fortifies my soul to know
That though I perish, truth is so:
That, howsoe'er I stray and range,
Whate'er I do, thou dost not change.
I steadier step when I recall
That if I slip, thou dost not fall.

Arthur Hugh Clough

I feel like a man who has no money in his pocket, but is allowed to draw for all he wants upon one infinitely rich. I am, therefore, at once both a beggar and a rich man.

John Newton, Out of the Depths

I went into the cathedral, which is really grand enough when one thinks of its antiquity and of the remoteness of the place; and at the end I offered up my adoration to God. I again addressed a few words to St Columba; and I warmed my soul with religious resolutions. I felt a kind of exultation in thinking that the solemn scenes of piety ever remain the same, though the cares and follies of life may prevent us from visiting them, or may even fancy that their effects were only 'as yesterday when it is past', and never again to be perceived. I hoped that ever after having been in this holy place I should maintain an exemplary conduct. One has a strange propensity to fix upon some point from whence a better course of life may be said to begin.

James Boswell, on a tour to Iona

Reconciliation – A South African Experience

M. Stanley Mogoba

The Christian Church throughout the world is challenged to bear witness to the lordship of Jesus Christ in their lives, their families, their country and in the world. In a world of conflict and violence, the ministry of reconciliation stands out as a beacon of hope.

South Africa has come through a very rough and worrying period. All analysts and prophets affirmed that we were standing on the edge of a cliff and that a blood bath was a certainty. It was a miracle that we made a turn-around and entered into negotiations for a new dispensation.

Some people say that we 'negotiated a revolution'. Ours is one of the countries in the world where the Church was persecuted but turned the situation round to become a significant mouthpiece of the voiceless people of our land. The 'turbulent priests' became a force to reckon with when they declared apartheid 'a heresy'.

Few people in the world have heard of a place called Rustenburg. It is a small town west of Pretoria, where an important ecumenical Conference of Church Leaders was held. It was a broadly-based gathering which spanned a very wide spectrum of Churches, widely separated by denominational and ideological circumstances.

The Rustenburg Conference re-discovered the word *forgiveness*. In the tense atmosphere of this Conference, an Afrikaner Dutch Reformed Minister, Professor Willie Jonker, confessed and asked forgiveness for his and his Church's involvement in apartheid. This confession was epochal. South Africa was never the same again.

The Rustenburg Declaration of November 1990 stated, *inter alia*:

> We, two hundred and thirty representatives of ninety-seven denominations and organisations ... have come together in Rustenburg in the belief that it is under the authority of God's Word and the guidance of the Holy Spirit . . . we had a strong sense that God was at work among us. We became aware that He was surprising us by His grace which cut through our fears and apprehensions . . .

This Rustenburg experience paved the way for a new South Africa. The subsequent Peace Conference and the Peace Accord was a direct result of Rustenburg as were the intense constitutional negotiations and the Government of National Unity.

We have come to realise that a country that was polarised by racial divisions, fear, suspicion and mistrust cannot be saved by more violence or guns or nuclear weapons. We have come to realise the strength and power that *forgiveness* and *reconciliation* have in our world. The picture of Nelson Mandela and F. W. de Klerk shaking hands spoke more eloquently than any words could express of the physical and spiritual energy in the hearts of human beings.

Prayer has also played an important part. Never before has our nation prayed in the way that it did for a peaceful change. Sports grounds which hold twenty to thirty thousand people were full of Christians in many parts of the country like Johannesburg, Durban and Cape Town. We experienced wonderful power from above and we knew that our land could never be the same again.

Thus was born a new type of democracy – a Christian, reconciling democracy – a democracy that seeks to bury the hurts and ugliness of the past; a democracy that enables the oppressor and the oppressed, the persecutor and the persecuted, the enemies in a war, to join hands and try to govern together; a democracy that accommodates minority groups and minority interests; a democracy that tries to merge different army formations into one national army; a democracy that tries to have one police force; a democracy that tries to have one educational system instead of fifteen systems, and so on.

Forgiveness and *reconciliation* together are indeed powerful and transforming. I am reminded of Coventry where nails from the devastated, burnt Cathedral were made into small crosses – two small charred nails, proclaiming hidden power – HE LIVES!

In conclusion, I repeat what I wrote elsewhere:

> The task of the Church for many years to come is going to be that of enabling polarised people with deep feelings of fear, hatred and distrust to find each other and live together in the same country. Reconciliation is a Christian word and concept. The world will never understand it if the Church does not preach it and live it. Without reconciliation, the best promises, the best agreements, the best constitutions, will remain mere words without any meaning, without any practical help to anybody.

O friends! with whom my feet have trod
    The quiet aisles of prayer,
Glad witness to your zeal for God
    And love of man I bear.

Yet, in the maddening maze of things,
    And tossed by storm and flood,
To one fixed trust my spirit clings;
    I know that God is good.

The wrong that pains my soul below
    I dare not throne above,
I know not of his hate — I know
    His goodness and his love.

I dimly guess from blessings known
    Of greater out of sight,
And, with the chastened Psalmist, own
    His judgements too are right.

I long for household voices gone,
    For vanished smiles I long,
But God hath led my dear ones on,
    And he can do no wrong.

I know not what the future hath
    Of marvel or surprise,
Assured alone that life and death
    His mercy underlies.

And if my heart and flesh are weak
  To bear an untried pain,
The bruisèd reed he will not break,
  But strengthen and sustain.

No offering of my own I have,
  Nor works my faith to prove;
I can but give the gifts he gave,
  And plead his love for love.

And so beside the Silent Sea
  I wait the muffled oar;
No harm from him can come to me
  On ocean or on shore.

I know not where his islands lift
  Their fronded palms in air;
I only know I cannot drift
  Beyond his love and care.

O brothers! if my faith is vain,
  If hopes like these betray,
Pray for me that my feet may gain
  The sure and safer way.

And thou, O Lord! by whom are seen
  Thy creatures as they be,
Forgive me if too close I lean
  My human heart on thee!

John Greenleaf Whittier

I have grown to believe that the one thing worth aiming at is simplicity of heart and life, that one's relations with others should be direct and not diplomatic; that power leaves a bitter taste in the mouth; that meanness, and hardness and coldness are the unforgivable sins; that conventionality is the mother of dreariness; that pleasure exists not in virtue of material conditions, but the joyful heart; that the world is a very interesting and beautiful place; that congenial labour is the secret of happiness; and many other things which seem, as I write them down, to be dull and trite commonplaces, but are for me the bright jewels which I have found beside the way.

A. C. Benson, *From a College Window*

All that Christians have is God in the centre of life, identified with man in Christ, drowning in the cruel sea of death and failure, revealing himself obscurely, ambiguously, so that we have to ask interminably what it all means and whether anything we say about him makes sense. At the cross he seems to be completely surrendered to man's freedom and destroyed by an angry and hateful world. But Christians see a deeper surrender there which gives an incalcuable weight of meaning to the cross. It is not difficult to believe in the presence of God in those places and events where life is conspicuously beautiful and happy. Christian faith, without denying or even doubting what is given us then, is deeply committed to the conviction that the kingdom of God comes, comes with power, in the kind of situation in which a man asks why he has been forsaken but does not himself abandon God.

J. Neville Ward, *Five for Sorrow, Ten for Joy*

Anyone who has recognised that the idea of Love is the spiritual beam of light which reaches us from the Infinite, ceases to demand from religion that it shall offer him complete knowledge of the suprasensible. He ponders indeed on the great questions; what is the meaning of evil in the world; how in God the First Cause, the will-to-create and the will-to-love are one; in what relation the spiritual and the material life stand to one another, and in what way our existence is transitory and yet eternal. But he is able to leave these questions on one side, however painful it may be to give up hope of answers to them. In the knowledge of spiritual existence in God through love he possesses the one thing needful – 'Love never faileth, but whether there be knowledge it shall be done away.'

Albert Schweitzer, *My Life and Thought*

We are in danger of drowning on the open sea, and God's word is the rope ladder thrown down to us so that we can climb up into the rescuing vessel. It is the carpet, rolled out toward us so that we can walk along it to the Father's throne. It is the lantern which shines in the darkness of the world (a world which keeps silence and refuses to reveal its own nature); it casts a softer light on the riddles which torment us and encourages us to keep going.

Hans Urs von Balthasar, *Prayer*

When trouble haunts me, need I sigh?
No, rather smile away despair;
For those have been more sad than I,
With burdens more than I could bear;
Aye, gone rejoicing under care
Where I had sunk in black despair.

When pain disturbs my peace and rest,
Am I a hopeless grief to keep,
When some have slept on torture's breast
And smiled as in the sweetest sleep,
Aye, peace on thorns, in faith forgiven,
And pillowed on the hope of heaven?

Though low and poor and broken down,
Am I to think myself distrest?
No, rather laugh where others frown
And think my being truly blest;
For others I can daily see
More worthy riches worse than me.

John Clare, The Stranger

To the man who himself strives earnestly, God also lends a helping hand.

Aeschylus

When I would beget content, and increase confidence in the power and wisdom and providence of Almighty God, I will walk the meadows of some gliding stream, and there contemplate the lilies that take no care, and those very many other little living creatures that are not only created, but fed (a man knows not how) by the goodness of the God of Nature, and therefore trust in him.

Izaak Walton

If you could crush the supernatural in the Bible, there remains yet a little task for you – you must crush it in the whole universe, and to do that you must crush the universe with it, for it exists everywhere, and its roots are in the foundation of all things.

William Howitt, *The History of the Supernatural*

'He humbled himself.' It is a thought as awful as it is full, as no other thought can be, of blessing and hope for the sons of men. But unless all that the Christian faith rests on is altogether baseless, nothing short of it is the truth. We need not fear to face it in all its reality. The Christian Scriptures never could have been written on any other faith, or any other conceivable basis of facts.

Dean Church, *Cathedral and University Sermons*

I believe in the immortality of the soul because I have within me immortal longings. I believe that the state we enter after death is wrought of our own motives, thoughts and deeds. I believe that in the life to come I shall have the senses I have not had here, and that my home there will be beautiful with colour, music and speech of flowers and faces I love.

Without this faith there would be little meaning in my life. I should be 'a mere pillar of darkness in the dark'. Observers in the full enjoyment of their bodily senses pity me, but it is because they do not see the golden chamber in my life where I dwell delighted; for, dark as my path may seem to them, I carry a magic light in my heart. Faith, the spiritual strong searchlight, illumines the way, and although sinister doubts lurk in the shadow, I walk unafraid towards the Enchanted Wood where the foliage is always green, where joy abides, where nightingales nest and sing, and where life and death are one in the Presence of the Lord.

Helen Keller

Treasures New and Old

Alan Beith

I like the picture which Jesus paints of the householder who brings forth from his treasure 'things new and old'. A year book is a good time to bring out such treasures, and I intend to claim the privilege of digging out some of the older treasures from the Methodist store, lest they be forgotten. They are a strange mixture, but they are real treasures to be set alongside the new.

The first is audible; the second is tangible and visible; the third is edible – yes, edible; and the last defies categorisation.

What is audible? It is singing and, more particularly, that uniquely powerful and compelling experience of four-part harmony sung by a substantial mixed congregation. This has nothing to do with the rather artificial argument between new songs and old hymns: there is plenty of room for both, and the editors of *Hymns & Psalms* wisely accepted that if such diversity means a sizeable hymn book, so be it. It means extra song sheets as well. But please can we have music copies, with harmony, and learn to use them? It is not that the gospel writers added an extra commandment – 'thou shalt sing in four parts': it is simply that Methodism has discovered an amazing power in this kind of singing.

The Conference, as well as practising the skills of singing, has preached them: in 1796 Conference decreed, 'Let the women constantly sing their parts alone. Let no man sing with them unless he understands the notes and sings the bass.' In the last century and for much of this, Welsh congregations studied the tonic sol-fa system; school music teaching, until it was hit by cuts, was beginning to make staff notation available to many more young people. Youth choirs as well as mixed and male voice choirs provided training for a minority, but we no longer convert that into a general practice of congregational part-singing. We will lose a great treasure if we do not restore it.

What is tangible and visible? The heritage of buildings which Methodism has produced, which are increasingly recognised by the wider community for the contribution they make to the townscape, and for their internal dignity and charm. We could never have sustained the huge inheritance of over-building which marked the nineteenth century, and some buildings have had to be adapted to enable them to 'serve the present age'.

But the present age, and future ages, will also be better served if we make certain that we conserve some of the best of our remaining buildings, and if we guard against vandalism in dealing with the most interesting and attractive interiors. A fine mahogany pulpit or a dignified set of pews can remain just as fitting for worship as a 'remodelled sanctuary' which will date very quickly. There is a danger in exaggerating the evangelical power of the fitted carpet and the spiritual qualities of the stacking chair. Where especially valuable chapels are no longer needed or practical, we now have a means of preserving them through the Historic Chapels Trust, on which I serve.

What is edible? Everything that is laid out on the creaking tables of a chapel supper. The fellowship of the tea table is a curiously powerful element in Methodist experience. I remember a minister who controversially, but convincingly, asserted that there was a more real sense of the Lord's Supper as a family meal when the congregation and friends were gathered round the tea tables at a Chapel Anniversary than in some of the formal Communion Services he had attended. The notion of hospitality, of a ready welcome symbolised by a well-laid table, runs right through Jesus' parables and ministry. Methodists readily recognised how much more easily some people could be brought into fellowship in the informality of the meal, and it is a treasure not to be lost.

And what defies any of these categories? It is simplicity. Some people search for ceremony, formality and theatre in worship, and the capacity of these things to serve as vehicles for worship is proven in their own experience. But others are put off by these things, and look for the simple treasures. In my Methodist youth we hardly ever saw a Minister preach other than in an ordinary suit – it would have to be somebody very grand from the theological college for even a plain gown to be seen. Nor did we ever repeat words from a service-book or often hear a preacher read a prayer.

With some Ministers dressing as if they are auditioning for an opera chorus, and some services requiring the congregation to read so many responses that you dare not close your eyes for a moment's real meditation, the treasure of simplicity is especially welcome, and happily still to be found here and there in Methodism. The Covenant Service is sometimes taken to be Methodism's only distinctive contribution to liturgy: the words which form the core of it are deeply challenging and beautiful, but it is not this annual formal service but the simplicity of the plain preaching service which most people remember as characteristic of Methodist worship.

Do we need these old things, when there are so many new things, new gifts of the Spirit?

The householder who brings out only the old treasures and none of the new will fail: but so will the householder who brings out only the new. Some of Methodism's older treasures deserve to be got out and polished.

Child of My love, fear not the unknown morrow,
Dread not the new demand life makes of thee
Thy ignorance doth hold no cause for sorrow
Since what thou knowest not is known to Me.

Thou canst not see today the hidden meaning
Of My command, but thou the light shalt gain
Walk on in faith, upon My promise leaning,
And as thou goest all shall be made plain.

One step thou seest — then go forward boldly,
One step is far enough for faith to see
Take that, and thy next duty shall be told thee,
For step by step the Lord is leading thee.

Stand not in fear, thy adversaries counting,
Dare every peril, save to disobey
Thou shalt march on, all obstacles surmounting,
For I, the strong, will open up the way.

Wherefore go gladly to the task assigned thee,
Having My promise, needing nothing more
Than just to know, where'ere the future find thee,
In all thy journeying I go before.

Frank J Exley, Child of My Love

We believe that the power behind us is greater than the task ahead.

Motto over a church in Missouri

> God shall be my hope,
> My stay, my guide and lantern to my feet.
>
> *William Shakespeare*

There is but one way to tranquillity of mind and happiness. Let this therefore be always ready at hand with thee, both when thou wakest early in the morning, and when thou goest late to sleep, to account no external thing thine own, but commit all these to God.

Epictetus

A person consists of his faith. Whatever is his faith, even so is he.

Hindu proverb

I have some favourite flowers in spring, among which are the mountain daisy, the harebell, the foxglove, the wild briar rose, the budding birch and the hoary hawthorn, that I view and hang over with particular delight. I never hear the loud solitary whistle of the curlew in a summer noon, or the wild mixing cadence of a troop of grey plovers without feeling an elevation of soul like the enthusiasm of devotion or poetry. Tell me to what this can be owing? ... I own myself partial to such proofs of those awful and important realities – a God that made all things – man's immaterial and immortal nature – and a world of weal and woe beyond the grave.

Robert Burns

O high and glorious God,
enlighten my heart.
Give me unwavering faith,
sure hope,
and perfect love.
Give me deep humility,
wisdom, and knowledge,
that I may keep your commandments. Amen.

Carlo Carretto, I, Francis

God forbid that I should measure the immensity of God's love by the
narrow limits of my own capacity for faith and hope.

St Bernard of Clairvaux

Night was come, and her planets were risen; a safe still night; too serene for the companionship of fear. We know that God is everywhere; but certainly we feel his presence most when his works are on the grandest scale spread before us; and it is in the unclouded night sky where his worlds wheel their silent course, that we read clearest his infinitude, his omnipotence, his omnipresence. I had risen from my knees to pray for Mr Rochester. Looking up, I, with tear dimmed eyes, saw the mighty Milky Way, remembering what it was – what countless systems there swept space like a soft trace of light – I felt the might and strength of God.

Charlotte Brontë, *Jane Eyre*

Almighty Father, Thy love is like a great sea that girdles the earth. Out of the deep we come to float awhile upon its surface. We cannot sound its depth nor tell its greatness, only we know it never faileth. The winds that blow over us are the breathing of Thy Spirit; the sun that lights and warms us is Thy truth. Now Thou does suffer us to sail calm seas; now Thou dost buffet us with storms of trouble; on the crest of waves of sorrow Thou dost raise us, but it is Thy love that bears us up; in the trough of desolation Thou dost sink us, that we may see nought but Thy love on every side. And when we pass into the deep again the waters of Thy love encompass and enfold us. The foolish call them the waters of misery and death; those who have heard the whisper of Thy Spirit know them for the boundless ocean of eternal life and love.

Anonymous

Then I remembered the faith that I have partly expressed, faith in a universe not measured by our fears, a universe that has thought and more than thought inside of it, and as I gazed, after the sunset and above the electric lights there shone the stars.

Oliver Wendell Holmes Jr, *The Mind and Faith of Justice*

Reconciliation

Emilio Castro

After having visited townships, hospitals and bereaved families in South Africa, after having come face to face with the reality of the blind violence which continues to exact more and more sacrifice from the same poor, marginalised and powerless people who have been paying the price of apartheid for many years, one needs to be very courageous to speak about reconciliation.

Or when one thinks of Latin America, where the Indians were destroyed by the invasion and occupation 500 years ago, and black Africans were brought as slaves to replace the dying Indian population in the cane sugar plantations, how does one talk about reconciliation?

But what, then, shall we do with the gospel of Jesus Christ, which obliges us to believe in reconciliation? That is our difficulty. If we could only set aside the heritage of historic power relationships – the history of white people being the guardians of blacks in South Africa, the history of colonisers and colonised Latin America and elsewhere in the world – we might solve the problem of reconciliation. But of course we cannot escape from history so easily.

As Christians we believe that God was in Christ to reconcile the world to himself, and that God has entrusted to us a ministry of reconciliation. We may have different doctrinal interpretations of the cross of

Jesus Christ, but all currents of Christian spirituality coincide in seeing the cross as God's ultimate attempt to overcome human alienation. And on that cross, from the side of the victims and in identification with the oppressed, Jesus pronounced the words of forgiveness: 'Father, forgive them, for they know not what they do.'

So this is our dilemma: a reality that makes reconciliation impossible and a vision, a conviction, a promise and an obligation that make reconciliation available. How do we bridge the gap between the vision and the reality?

Theologically we might put it this way. In the case of Jesus Christ, he as the victim was able to mediate restitution and forgiveness, even for those who had victimised him. 'Father, forgive them, for they know not what they do.' So, too, the father's embrace of the Prodigal Son and Esau's embrace of Jacob represent a giving back of a lost humanness, which can only be given through the victim, and which is fundamental if reconciliation is to take place.

In the recent political debate in South Africa, there has been a good deal of talk about how restitution, a means by which those who were responsible for the situation, those who have profited from apartheid, the guilty ones, can be obliged to pay the others back for what they have suffered, is necessary in order for it to be possible to begin to talk about reconciliation.

But the victim is not only a recipient of restitution. The victim is also the one who has the key to a real and fundamental reconciliation, because it is in the victim that Jesus Christ is present. It is in these people that God's intention for real humanness is manifested. So reconciliation comes at the end of a road, after you have taken steps, from different motivations, after you have come close to your neighbour, in relation to whom you recognise your guilt, after you have begun to give an indication of the seriousness of your approach. When you are embraced by those who are your former victims, then there is a chance for real building of a new fellowship, a new communion and a new community.

Of course, it is not a simple matter to move from the biblical, theological context to the contemporary political sense. In the Bible, with some exceptions, conflict and reconciliation take place in a face-to-face situation between individuals. And that is relatively easy to grasp: 'I could forgive him' – and vice versa. It is quite different when I belong to a social group that has been collectively guilty or collectively exploited. My attitude of individual forgiveness is not enough and is not complete until I come along with my family or my people to that possibility of reconciliation.

A senior ecumenical leader has said, 'I don't have any problems accepting forgiveness of my own sins. But I do not know how to accept forgiveness for my sin of being white, of being a member of a racial group that has profited from the exploitation of so many other nations in the world, and continues to profit from the structure of economic relations in the world. How can I accept forgiveness when the cause of my sin, the sin of my nation as a whole, is still in operation?'

The only response is to begin to walk like Jacob, like the Prodigal Son. Come with your guilt, but let us put ourselves on the side of the downtrodden, on the side of the marginalised, in order to try to reverse the meaning of history. We cannot change past history, but we can change the significance of that history for this and future generations.

We must come to the question of restitution. As we can see from biblical accounts, restitution is a sign of the honesty of the process. Restitution is a way to guarantee and protect life, to prove your honesty and to facilitate others' perception of the honesty of your position. But restitution is also something deeper. It is the conviction that we cannot say 'We have finished a page, so now we begin again from zero', without assuming the consequences from the past and creating conditions of humanness for everyone.

At one African National Congress seminar someone proposed that a tax of 30 per cent be levied on wealth to compensate somehow for the disadvantages of the majority of the people. The resulting uproar in the media demonstrated two things: that some people in South Africa are afraid of losing their privileges and that others are convinced that something needs to be done. The point is to internalise that conviction and to bring that internalisation to the negotiating tables. The issue is not whether this or that idea should be accepted or rejected but to bring forward intelligent possibilities that will indicate a willingness to make restitution and to explore the possibilities involved in the process of creating conditions for a real reconciliation.

What is the role of the church in all this? Its first task is to shout very loudly, 'Reconciliation is possible! Do not give up! Do not surrender to violence! Reject the idea that violence can be a methodology to remove or to maintain the status quo!' Such a No to violence is needed because the promise of reconciliation is there, and we believe that God's promises are stronger than our human obstacles to their fulfillment.

Second, let the church be close to the victims, to the suffering people, to keep steadying them with the hope that, even if death visits us today, it is not powerful enough to deprive those who have fallen on the road of the glory of contemplating, from the outskirts of heaven, how the life of their dear ones is being transformed for the better. That is where the church must be because it is from that perspective, and with the hope generated in that encounter with the people, that others can be embraced in a sincere and honest manner.

Finally, let the church set up signs of the potential of reconciliation by running a little faster than civil society and providing examples of potential encounters on the road to reconciliation. It cannot be that churches will change because the political parties change. It cannot be that the dreams the churches can develop are limited to the possibilities that politicians have for fulfilling them. No, the church must say in the name of our God, 'Reconciliation is waiting for us. Let us begin to assure life. Let us begin to walk to the encounter with our neighbour. Let us begin to make restitution. Let us hope for the miracle that will surprise us at any moment.'

Give me to be thy child, and learn for ever at thy knee.
Give me to grow weak and grey-headed, since thou willst it so.
Bid me aside
Lay all the pleasures of my youth and pride,
Gladness as well,
Sweet ardours and bright hopes – I'll not rebel.

Only, I pray, keep me beside thee all the night and day,
Only for all thou takest give thyself and past recall!
And when youth's gone
As men count going, twixt us two alone
Still let me be
Thy little child, left learning at thy knee.

Anonymous

My Friends: No one, not in my situation, can appreciate my feeling of sadness at this parting. To this place, and the kindness of these people, I owe everything. Here I have lived a quarter of a century, and have passed from a young to an old man. Here my children have been born and one is buried. I now leave, not knowing when or whether I may return, with a task before me greater than that which rested upon Washington. Without the assistance of that Divine Being who ever attended him, I cannot succeed. With that assistance, I cannot fail. Trusting in him who can go with me, and remain with you, and be everywhere for good, let us confidently hope that all will yet be well.

Abraham Lincoln

COMPASSION
&
FORGIVENESS

Goodness is something so simple:
always to live for others,
never to seek one's own advantage.

Dag Hammarskjöld, Markings

Grant, O Lord, that in all the joys of life we may never forget to be kind. Help us to be unselfish in friendship, thoughtful of those less happy than ourselves, and eager to bear the burdens of others.

Charles L. Slattery

Adversity not only draws people together but brings forth that beautiful inward friendship, just as the cold winter forms ice figures on the window panes which the warmth of the sun effaces.

Soren Kierkegaard

Deeply sympathising with the inhabitants of Silfield, I sallied forth in the snow on Saturday and having obtained from a farmer the names of the more distressed, I have this day been supplying their wants... I gave to each about five shillings in clothing.

Rev. W. W. Andrew, *Diary*, 21st December, 1840

To ask that one's higher self should forgive one's own trespasses is the hardest prayer that we can ever offer up . . . We cannot forgive others in any comprehensible sense unless we have first learnt how to forgive ourselves.

Havelock Ellis, Selected Essays

God Brings People Together

Jean Vanier

We live in a society where many people feel lonely. Relationships are often difficult; places of belonging are broken. Loneliness brings with it anguish, a feeling of emptiness which tends to evolve into a sense of guilt: 'If I am not loved and wanted it is because I am no good.' Loneliness also brings the need to prove one's worth, sometimes in an aggressive way or in a form of depression. It creates an emptiness which we try to fill with work, distractions or even travel. Loneliness and boredom can be the source of much violence. People try to hide loneliness behind solid defence barriers, protecting themselves from the pain of anguish.

Jesus came to bond people together in love, so that each person can rise up from the pit of loneliness and meet others, communicate and share with them. Masks and defence mechanisms which hide the true self can fall, since people no longer need to pretend to be other than they are. Instead they are free to be themselves because they know they are loved.

We all yearn to love and be loved, yet we are frightened of love. Love is dangerous. If we begin to share with someone in need, we risk losing something: our time, our money, our goods, maybe even our autonomy. To love is to become vulnerable. We open our heart to others; we offer them our secret. But trust and friendship can be broken and are always broken by death. The loss of friendship plunges us deeper into anguish. The more we love the greater the pain.

Community is a network of love and of friendship which implies a certain commitment to others. We become responsible for them and they for us. Trust grows between us.

Community means walking in the same direction with others who share similar ideas, hopes and beliefs; it involves working together for the same goals. Community also means concern, love, caring for each person, for their growth in inner peace, happiness and well-being. Community is family. It is formed by people coming together to pray, to share and to work together. Sports, games, or social activities can also serve as the focal point to build community, as long as there is personal contact and a sense of caring between people.

Community is beautiful and liberating, but it is demanding as well. It implies that each is making the passage from 'the community for me' to 'me for the community'. It is a place of security for each person, where each is cared for, but it also means that each one cares for others, opening up to them, listening and understanding them. This can be difficult when others appear so different and are particularly in need; when they have temperaments which appear closed, depressed or aggressive. It means that we go beyond all the hurts and fears in people's lives and are able to see their intrinsic beauty and value. Love is not first and foremost to do things for others, but to reveal to them how valuable and precious they are. Through love we touch the places in others where their potential for growth in love or their potential for transformation and conversion are found.

Living in community with people who have disabilities, particularly learning difficulties, I have discovered how much community is liberating as well as threatening. How much it implies real effort and a new strength given by Jesus. It means that each one is being nourished in their mind, heart and motivations. It means that day after day people are choosing love and life rather than rejection, indifference and closedness.

I started l'Arche in 1964, when I welcomed Raphael and Philippe from a rather dismal institution. Both had severe learning difficulties and had been put in the asylum when their parents died. They were depressed, angry and lonely when they came to live with me in a small, rather dilapidated house I had bought in a small village in northern France. But they were happy to be out of the asylum. Living together was simple and wonderful but also difficult for them, as well as for me! It took time to get to know each other. We had to discover what community was all about and how to gradually move out of the prisons of fear and self-centredness that are in us. They had to risk opening up to life and to love. I had to take the risk of listening and serving rather than trying to dominate and control. We all need to be changed!

Now, thirty years later, that first community has grown. There are now about four hundred of us living in many little houses, scattered among nearby villages. And from that first community over one hundred other communities have grown in twenty-eight countries, (seven in the U.K.), each with the same vision and spirit. We are building community together, people with learning disabilities and those who have come to join them. We are discovering how the weak person is capable of awakening the hearts of those who are stronger and more efficient, leading them on the path of love and compassion to the heart of the Gospel message.

About six years ago we welcomed Antonio, a young man of twenty-six who is extremely fragile. He cannot walk or speak or use his hands. His body is small and crippled. Yet when you approach him and call him by name, his whole face lights up and a smile breaks out. Peace and trust flow from his gentle, wounded body. There is no trace of anger or depression in his bright eyes, just acceptance and transparency. Assistants who are close to him have told me: 'Antonio has transformed me.' Like most young people, they come from competitive backgrounds filled with conflict where people must be aggressive or defensive in order to protect themselves and to succeed. Antonio leads them into another world, the one of tenderness and gentleness. To give Antonio a bath, one cannot be in a hurry. One must be centred and peaceful. There is a healing power in Antonio, as in little children.

That does not mean that everything is easy for assistants with Antonio. It is demanding to be with people like him, for their needs are great. God hears the cry of the poor and the powerless but often their cry disturbs us; we do not want to hear it; we want to do our own thing in our own good time. And, of course, it is not always as gratifying to be with people with learning disabilities as with Antonio. Some are quite disturbed and carry with them a lot of anguish, anger and inner pain. This awakens our own anguish and inner pain, particularly when they refuse to co-operate and insist on remaining behind their walls of depression.

Living with people with learning disabilities, creating family and community with them, is not always simple, but many people have said how much they have been changed by them and have been brought into a world of love and of community by them. Our world needs communities that are open and welcoming, communities that reveal our brokenness, fears and barriers and lead us on a road to inner healing and wholeness.

In Luke 14 Jesus says:

> When you give a meal, do not invite members of your family, or your rich neighbours or your friends. When you give a party, invite the poor, the lame, the crippled and the blind and you shall be blessed.

This is one of the founding texts of l'Arche. We are discovering how blessed we are. Many assistants could have climbed the ladder of power and success if they had not come to l'Arche. But Jesus called them to climb down the ladder into the sea of love and of commitment. They became friends of those who were rejected, put aside, considered as useless and through this they have discovered that love heals in a way that social success cannot.

The work of God is to bring people together in love, to open their hearts in mutual respect and caring. The work of the evil spirit is to divide, to create barriers of indifference, prejudice and hatred, which create oppression, elimination and death. Community is the work of God; Bosnia is the work of the evil one. However, it is not always easy to hear Jesus calling us out of our fears, our self-centredness and personal projects in order to walk with him on the road of love and peace-making. If we agree to take this road, he gives us a new strength; he gives his Spirit. Gradually he changes our hearts of stone into hearts of flesh.

You cannot command or compel people into holiness, you cannot increase their spiritual stature one cubit by any kind of force or compulsion. You can do it only by sharing your life with them, by making them feel your goodness, by your love and sacrifice for them.

Rufus M. Jones, *The Double Search*

To the forgiveness of others three considerations have especially invited me:

1. That he that cannot forgive others breaks the bridge over which he must pass himself, for every man hath need to be forgiven.

2. That when a man wants or comes short of an entire and accomplished virtue, our defects may be supplied this way, since the forgiving of evil deeds in others amounteth to no less than virtue in us; that therefore it may be not unaptly called the paying our debts with another man's money.

3. That it is the most necessary and proper work of every man; for, though when I do not a just thing, or a charitable, or a wise, another man may do it for me, yet no man can forgive my enemy but myself.

I can truly say, nothing ever gave my mind more ease than when I had forgiven my enemies, which freed me from many cares and perturbations, which otherwise would have molested me.

Lord Herbert of Cherbury, *Autobiography*

O Lord, remember not only the men and women of goodwill but also those of illwill. But do not remember all the suffering they have inflicted on us; remember the fruits we bought, thanks to this suffering, our comradeship, our loyalty, our humility, the courage, the generosity, the greatness of heart which has grown out of this; and when they come to judgement, let all the fruits that we have borne be their forgiveness.

Prayer on a piece of wrapping paper found in Ravensbruck concentration camp for women.

Whoever is really brave has always this comfort when he is oppressed – that he knows himself to be superior to those who injure him: for the greatest power on earth can no sooner do him injury, but the brave man can make himself greater by forgiving it.

Alexander Pope

It is hard to find words in the language of men to explain the deep things of God. Indeed, there are none that will adequately express what the children of God experience. But perhaps one might say the testimony of the Spirit is an inward impression on the soul, whereby the Spirit of God directly witnesses to my spirit, that I am a child of God; that Jesus Christ hath loved me and given himself for me; and that all my sins are blotted out, and I, even I, am reconciled to God.

John Wesley

Reverence is a gentle virtue; it is also strong. Reverence is a tender virtue; it is also tough. Reverence is a patient virtue; it is also persistent. Reverence bears no ill will toward others; it is able to bear the ill will of others when necessary. Reverence is a virtue that prepares us well to belong to one another; it reaches out to those who have given messages of not wishing to belong.

When we approach others with gentle reverence, we bring gifts and share theirs with us.

Paula Ripple, *Growing Strong in Broken Places*

No person is kind only to one person at once, but to many persons in one.

F. W. Faber, Spiritual Conferences

God dwells among the lowliest of men. He sits on the dust heap among the prison convicts. With the juvenile delinquents he stands at the door, begging bread. He throngs with the beggars at the place of alms. He is among the sick. He stands in line with the unemployed in front of the free employment bureaux.

Therefore let him who would meet God visit the prison cell before going to the temple. Before he goes to church let him visit the hospital. Before he reads his Bible let him help the beggar standing at his door.

Toyohiko Kagawa, *Kagawa*, William Axling

This is the key of love, it openeth God's grace,
To comfort the sorrowful that are with sin entangled.
Love is the leech of life, next to our Lord,
It is the graft of grace, it is the nearest road to heaven.

Will Langland, Piers Plowman

Just as the sun shines and enlightens none the less brightly when I close my eyes, so this throne of grace, this forgiveness of sins, is always there, even though I fall. Just as I see the sun again when I open my eyes, so I have forgiveness and the sense of it once more when I look up and return to Christ. We are not to measure forgiveness as narrowly as fools dream.

Martin Luther

A healthy forgetter is developed by forgiveness. We cannot erase the memory cards of our failures in our brain computer until we have a profound experience of forgiveness. The authentic mark of truly mature persons is the capacity to forgive themselves. But that is a rare commodity. Years of experience of seeking to be a whole person and helping others with their self-esteem has led me to the conclusion that one of the greatest miracles of life is self-forgiveness. I have never known a person who has been able to do it without a healing experience of Christ's kindness.

Lloyd John Ogilvie, *Radiance of the Inner Splendour*

143

A young boy was brought to my house to sweep the copper chimney, which runs nearly perpendicular to the top of the house, and is about a brick and a half in width, and pretty nearly square, so that its dimensions may easily be ascertained; there was a hole made in the side for the boy to go up, and the boy was repeatedly driven in at the hole, but the mortar and soot fell in such great lumps on his head, that if he had not had a cap upon his head it would have been broken. Upon seeing the boy writhing in order to get up the chimney, and being satisfied he could not conveniently get up, although the man who was his master seemed to say it was mere idleness in the boy, and that he would force the boy up, I would not suffer it, and the chimney was not swept.

George Reveley, *Parliamentary Enquiry on Climbing Boys, 1817*

Heirs to Peter's Misunderstanding

Rosemary Wakelin

The issue of women and the Church has been a bit like a volcano erupting. An enormous amount of debris has been flung out and it has by no means settled. But it may now be possible to sift through the rubble and try to find some sort of order in the new topography. I want to try to do this in the light of the reconciling Christ, in whom there is neither male nor female, who restored the lost balance of trust and control and enabled us to see what God is like and what humanity should be like.

The social arguments that cloud the issue tend to be around the area of rights and equality. Of course these matter and have political, legal and theological importance, but putting them right is cosmetic compared with tackling the roots of the problem which they camouflage. The theological arguments are more sinister, although they begin with the human fear of vulnerability and hunger for acquiring and keeping power, and then root themselves deeply in Judaism, Church history and psychological dis-ease. It could be that the denigrating of women and the persistent rejection of the feminine in God and of the image of God in women, which arises from this dis-ease, has helped to produce our violent history and the divisions which still tear us apart.

Suspicion, fear and even hatred of the feminine lie just below the surface in society and the Church, and are of deeper significance than perhaps we realise. Women encounter this antagonism in a thousand different ways – particularly as they emerge from traditional roles and assume responsibilities outside the home. Some men, whose nature and skills are in areas more associated with women, come under attack – because femaleness is perceived as weak and sub-standard: maleness – of a particular sort – is the preferred norm. We may pay lip service to the belief that men and women are made in God's image, but our history suggests that we have preferred the male image and have discouraged any exploration of the female image and its implications. It often seems that we have made God in a man's image, and by doing so we have produced a distorted image of God, of humanity and human society.

By denigrating the 'feminine' to an inferior status we have rejected the other way of being human, of understanding how things work, solving problems and the wisdom arising from the complementarity of roles. By grossly exaggerating the importance of male attributes like dominance, aggression, competitiveness and power-seeking, we have brought ourselves to the possibility of Mutually Assured Destruction. The Church jumped on to this power bandwagon – originally when Constantine made the Church safe and respectable. The medieval Church was colossally powerful and engaged in all the usual political and military struggles and aggrandisement of any empire. Since the Reformation this power has slowly declined, giving place to denominational posturing and internecine scraps which may lose their significance as the ecumenical movement gathers credibility. Perhaps God is giving us a second chance.

John's Gospel has Jesus saying, 'When you have seen me you have seen the Father.' So we look at Jesus and 'see' what God is like in the evidence of the Gospels.

The birth stories let us see a God prepared to be vulnerable and recognised, not by the powerful, but by people beyond the pale. The Temptations are about God in Christ looking at methods and strategies to establish his new community, and firmly rejecting three archetypal ways, all involving power as the world understands it, choosing to use not the love of power but the Power of Love – which means vulnerability. What then follows is the story of how, in Christ, he did do it. The Gospels show Jesus very much in control but using his power to heal, teach, affirm, build relationships and verbally attack the powerful people whose control put up barriers between people and God. He seems to have resisted any attempt to be in a powerful position, 'know the right people' or manipulate God's power to establish his own position.

Trusting that 'love works', Jesus used his male human attributes – his aggression, initiative, assertiveness – not to control people, as they are usually used, but to release his female human attributes of enabling, nourishing and sustaining them in understanding and growing in his idea of what life is for, which carried the possibility of becoming a victim. He redefined what it means to be a man, a woman and God. Women, institutionally excluded by Jewish law from any function outside the home, were, by Jesus, included in the new Community. Disregarded children became the most important. Outcasts – for whatever reason – were brought within the fold. Jesus was not a feminist. He merely threw out all the reasons for exclusion and offered membership of the Kingdom to everyone – which inevitably affected women whose natural bodily functions had meant that for a good percentage of their lives they were 'unclean'. By claiming and using the 'feminine' attributes in himself, he restored the lost balance of God's image in humanity and at last presented what had been intended – the perfect humanity, control and trust in balance, the paradox of strength in vulnerability. And so we see what God is like.

Being a woman in the Church, studying Church History and belonging to the first generation of women who have had some say in what to do with their lives and some control over their reproduction, I have become more and more convinced that the Church as an institution has failed to be the body of Christ. The reason for its survival is that there have always been individuals and groups who have been 'the Church' in particular situations, and because the Church is of Divine origin, it belongs to God and God has not yet given up on it.

Peter's story in the Gospels maps out rather neatly where things went wrong. He lived in an occupied land and longed for Jewish sovereignty, and he was fired by prophecies of a messiah. So when Jesus asked his disciples who they thought he was, Peter came up with the right answer. Matthew's Gospel has Jesus enthusiastically affirming Peter for receiving a God-given insight, and going on to commission him with all sorts of authority and power. Jesus then spelt out that being Messiah in his agenda meant being rejected and put to death. But Peter had an agenda of his own – messiahship meant power as we understand it. He rebuked Jesus and in return received a stinging rebuke. His thoughts were no longer God-inspired. The history of the institutional Church suggests that the first part of the story has been noted and the second part ignored – it has latched on to Peter's agenda not Jesus'. Cross-bearing has been the prerogative of the 'real' Church that has always been a minority. Key-holding and authority have been the preferred option of the institutional Church.

The rejection by the Church of the implications of that story is more remarkable when put alongside the story in John's Gospel of Peter's re-instatement and re-commissioning. The chance to reverse the three denials is graciously given and humbly, if uncomfortably, accepted. And then Peter is given his new role. Nothing about keys or authority – but plenty about tending and feeding, followed by the alarming information that he will not be in control, but that like Jesus he, too, will become a victim.

Maybe the Church, like Peter, has had to pass through a long misunderstanding struggling to be faithful to Christ while locked firmly into very worldly, male power structures. Key bearing still seems to be a more promising option than cross-carrying, an Almighty God a more suitable ally than a young man strung up on a gibbet. Do we actually want a God who is vulnerable? According to the New Testament that is God's secret wisdom. We still have terrible moments of denial. Maybe Christ is asking us again if we really love him – which is what it comes down to. Perhaps, like Peter, we find it hard to reply. But when we do we are given the same commission – to tend and feed and to be willing to share the vulnerability of love and actually trust that God can cope. This needs all the controlling, brave initiative of our maleness and all the trusting, courageous acceptance of our femaleness. 'Here am I, send me,' and, 'I am the Lord's servant, may it be as you have said.'

Have I rejoiced with and for my neighbour in virtue or pleasure? Grieved with him (her) in pain, for him in sin?

Have I received his infirmities with pity, not anger?

Have I thought or spoken unkindly of or to him?

Have I revealed any evil of anyone, unless it was necessary to some particular good I had in view? Have I then done it with all the tenderness of phrase and manner consistent with that end? Have I anyway appeared to approve them that did otherwise?

Has goodwill been, and appeared to be, the spring of all my actions toward others?

Have I duly used intercession? Before, after, speaking to any? For my friends on Sunday? For my pupils on Monday? For those who have particularly desired it, on Wednesday and Friday? For the family in which I am, every day?

John Wesley

This country town hospital is differently regarded by the villagers of the Plain. It is curious to find how many among them are personally acquainted with it; perhaps it is not easy for anyone, even in this most healthy district, to get through life without sickness, and all are liable to accidents. The injured or afflicted youth, taken straight from his rough, hard life and poor cottage, wonders at the place he finds himself in – the wide, clean, airy room and white easy bed, the care and skill of the doctors, the tender nursing of women, and comforts and luxuries, all without payment, but given as it seems to him out of pure divine love and compassion – all this comes to him as something strange, almost incredible. He suffers much perhaps, but can bear pain stoically and forget it when it is past, but the loving kindness he has experienced is remembered.

W. H. Hudson, *A Shepherd's Life*

All that we are is the result of what we have thought: it is founded on our thoughts, it is made up of our thoughts. If a man speaks or acts with evil thought, pain follows him, as the wheel follows the foot of the ox that draws the carriage.

All that we are is the result of what we have thought: it is founded on our thoughts, it is made up of our thoughts. If a man speaks or acts with a pure thought, happiness follows him, like a shadow that never leaves him.

'He abused me, he beat me, he defeated me, he robbed me' — in those who harbour such thoughts hatred will never cease.

For hatred does not cease by hatred at any time: hatred ceases by love — this is an old rule.

The world does not know that we must all come to an end here; but those who know it, their quarrels cease at once.

Gotama Buddha

Democracy

An Implication for the Methodist Church in Aotearoa – New Zealand

Stanley J. West

Democracy is a word that has taken on a particular meaning for the Methodist Church of New Zealand, Te Haahi Weteriana o Aotearoa. This is the result of a deliberate decision made by the Conference to face up to the issues of power sharing. Subsequently the Church has put in place a number of processes that encourage partnership and power sharing between Taha Maori (the original people) and Tauiwi (those who came after – ie European, Samoan, Tongan, Fijian).

For our Church the starting point is the Treaty of Waitangi which was signed in 1840, and understood by many to be the founding document of this nation. This Treaty document gave to new immigrants the right to live in this country, as well as ensuring that certain rights and responsibilities remained with Maori. History clearly shows that soon after its signing and in subsequent years the Treaty has not been honoured which has meant that Maori have been significantly disadvantaged. It was in choosing to address some of these wrongs that the Church made the decision, in 1983, to work towards becoming a bi-cultural Church which would reflect true partnership and power sharing.

To begin this process a Bi-Cultural Committee was set up, and was given the task of raising the bi-cultural questions with Committees, Boards and Parishes. Since then we have engaged in planning, training events and workshops and have consciously raised questions about our bi-cultural processes. In addition we have asked all those parts of the Church who hold property to undertake a review of the history of their land, responding to questions about how the land was originally acquired and if proper and adequate payments were made for those purchases. There are many issues relating to the acquisition of land which raise continuing questions requiring further conversation.

Another question that also needed to be addressed was, how does our Church find ways of sharing power between two partners when there is a significant difference in philosophy and in the size of the two groups? It has, for example, been my experience that when there are participating groups of unequal size then it is nearly always the voice of the larger group that is heard, which controls and shapes decisions. While it may not be intended that this should happen, it does, and in the process the smaller group invariably feels put down and their particular point of view not heard.

In addition to relative size we have also focused on the fact that the 'Westminster' style of ordering the business of Conference and other meetings works well for those who know the system and are comfortable about being 'on their feet', but it is not helpful for others. In its place we have moved to a consensus style of decision making. This means that in our decision making process we engage in a conversation together and ultimately reach a point where a decision is made. We no longer require people to move and second a motion, people are not timed and may speak more than once; it is a process that relies on each person accepting responsibility for his or her own actions.

As part of this decision making process we also provide the opportunity for the two partners, Taha Maori and Tauiwi, to hold a caucus when there are matters of significant difference or important issues being discussed. This enables each of the partners to hold their own conversations and determine their own mind. Following a caucus each partner will report to each other, thus creating a situation where one voice speaks to one voice. If a common mind is expressed then a decision will be made. If it is not possible to reach a common mind then a decision will not be made. The size of one group as it speaks to the other is not important in this decision making process; rather, what is important is that each group speaks with one voice.

It has been my experience that this way of functioning allows for greater member participation and means less domination by a powerful few. The meetings are less formal and have a more relaxed air about them. It has enabled us to move a long way along the road towards a more democratic process in decision making which allows for a greater sharing of power.

Within the last couple of years our Church has replaced the Church Council with a Council of Conference. The membership of this committee is made up of ten people appointed by Taha Maori and ten appointed by Tauiwi. In this way the two partners not only hold equal power but are seen to be doing so, and as such serve to form a visual example to the wider community of what can be possible. The responsibilities and tasks of the Council centre around the way we deploy and use both people and money resources of the Church, dealing with those matters that jointly affect both partners, envisioning and providing direction for our Church.

The significance of this new direction is that we have sought to provide a way for each to be equally involved in giving shape and direction to the life of our Church. This step has made it possible for Taha Maori to have greater control over things Maori and for Tauiwi to have control over those areas that relate to them. This change reflects a significant shift in power and the way in which decisions are reached.

Conclusion

I would not wish to imply that the bi-cultural journey has been easy for Te Haahi Weteriana, or that it has always had the full support of the various sections of the Church. But despite the hesitations of some, over these ten years there have occurred significant and important changes and I believe there would be few who would wish to revert completely back to the old. However, this journey like many is an on-going one; there is still a great deal of listening, learning, discovering and understanding that has yet to take place. For this reason one of the challenges to our Church and its members is to be found in the continuing pursuit of power sharing and in a better understanding of partnership.

I believe that what I have shared raises significant theological and personal questions about relationships, equality, caring and respect for one another, especially in the way we structure our Church life. We may choose structures that are exclusive and hurtful of others, or on the other hand we may choose structures that are open and inclusive. We do not always realise the effect our actions or processes can have upon others. Sometimes they can be supportive and caring but at other times they can be destructive and devaluing of others. Therefore, if we knowingly create or allow situations where others are put down, or their power is diminished then Christ is no longer present. I believe that this is true for the structures of the Church as much as it is for each of us individually. True democracy should be inclusive of all and reflect the mind that is in Christ.

'Ah, I was always too hard,' said Adam to himself, 'It's a sore fault in me that I'm hot and out of patience with people when they do wrong, and my heart gets shut up against 'em so as I can't bring myself to forgive 'em. I see clear enough that there's more pride nor love in my soul, for I could sooner make a thousand strokes with the hammer for my father than bring myself to say a kind word to him. Maybe the best thing I ever did in my life was only doing what was easiest for myself. It's allays been easier for me to work nor to sit still, but a real tough job for me 'ud be to master my own will and temper and go right against my own pride. It seems to me now, if I was to find father at home tonight, I should behave different; but there's no knowing — perhaps nothing 'ud be a lesson to us if it didn't come too late.'

George Eliot, Adam Bede
(reflecting on the recent death of his father)

The immediate circumstance which led my attention to the facts was a communication made to me by a very opulent spinner, that it was the regular custom to work children in factories thirteen hours a day, and only allow them half an hour for dinner; that that was the regular custom, and that in many factories they were worked considerably more . . . I resolved from that moment that I would dedicate every power of body and mind to this object, until these poor children were relieved from that excessive labour, and from that moment, which was the 29th of September 1830, I have never ceased to use every legal means . . . for the purpose of emancipating these innocent slaves.

Richard Oastler, Parliamentary Enquiry, 1832

DOUBT
&
HOPE

*I must understand in order that I
may believe. By doubting we
come to questioning, and by
questioning we perceive the
truth.*

Peter Abelard

St Thomas was right to question hearsay evidence. He was wrong in not trusting, as Jesus did, the evidence he was born with. So was I. That is what Jesus was telling him, I believe, in the story related in the Gospel of St John. Can I accept that story, as true history? I do not know. But I can trust it as a parable, for the truth of parable is always in the present tense. It is by the parable, not by the history, that we are saved, even though the history be true. You can believe the history and not be saved. 'The devils believe also, and tremble,' Jesus said. They believed, but lacked the faith.

I am in no position to blame St Thomas. It is hard to be as tough as Jesus was: to have the faith that Jesus had; to create as boldly as Jesus did. It is hard even to believe that Jesus wanted us to do this. I was not encouraged to believe it, but I do now begin to.

Sydney Carter, *My Believing Bones*
from *The Two Way Clock*

This then have I learned at the ends of the earth that I am fallen short of the glory of God and that I am altogether corrupt and abominable and consequently my whole life; seeing it cannot be that an evil tree should bring forth good fruit . . . The faith I want is a sure trust and confidence in God that, through the merits of Christ, my sins are forgiven and I reconciled to the favour of God.

John Wesley, 29th February, 1738

The Glory of Hope

Paul Boateng

St Augustine reminds us that 'hope has two beautiful daughters. Their names are anger and courage; anger at the way things are and courage to see that they do not remain the way they are.' We as Christians are all too often strong on hope but much less comfortable about anger. Anger does have its place, however. Christ himself displayed anger. He was angry, for instance, about the greedy moneychangers in the Temple. The prophet Amos, too, was angry about injustice, including that injustice and hypocrisy perpetrated by the people of God, and raged righteously against it:

> Therefore because you trample on the poor and take from them levies of grain, you have built houses of hewn stone, but you shall not live in them; you have planted pleasant vineyards, but you shall not drink their wine. For I know how many are your transgressions, and how great are your sins – you who afflict the righteous, who take a bribe, and push aside the needy in the gate . . . seek good and not evil, that you may live; and so the Lord, the God of hosts, will be with you, just as you have said. Hate evil and love good, and establish justice in the gate.
>
> I hate, I despise your festivals, and I take no delight in your solemn assemblies. Even though you offer me your burnt offerings and

> grain offerings, I will not accept them ... Take
> away from me the noise of your songs; I will
> not listen to the melody of your harps. But let
> justice roll down like waters, and righteousness
> like an everflowing stream.
>
> Amos 5:11-15, 21-24

Why then should we not learn to recognise the role of
anger? Our religion and our services are empty
without a proper place for anger. I was vividly
reminded of this on the Sunday of the elections in
South Africa in April 1994. I went to worship, as
always when I am in Johannesburg, at the Central
Methodist Church. I remembered my first visit there at
the height of the state of emergency when every single
day members of the church were being harassed and
arrested. There was then, burning on the altar, a
candle surrounded by barbed wire. Even in the midst
of the darkness that surrounded it, that light would not
be extinguished, but the source of pain had to be torn
down.

We might have expected on that happy Sunday, in the
aftermath of the first full and free elections in which
white and black had queued for hours together under
the hot sun in order to cast their hard-won vote, that
the barbed wire could at last be removed.

Not a bit of it. The Minister reminded us that morning
of all that was still to be done: the houses that were yet
to be built; the jobs that were still to be created; the
wounds to be healed. The wire was to remain. Even at
what might have appeared to be the ultimate moment
of victory there was still a cause to remain dissatisfied.

The dissatisfaction is not a denial of the promise of our
Christian faith, but rather a means of fulfilling it.
There are times inevitably in a political life when one

162

grows weary of the ritual, and at times synthetic, manifestation of anger across the Chamber of the House of Commons. There is a certain cure, however, for that weariness. I only have to open a filing cabinet in my office or open the doors of one of my Saturday morning Constituency Surgeries to be re-affirmed in my political convictions. There has to be a better way. Our society, our world and our people, created as we are in the image of God, surely deserve better than abject subjugation to mechanistic market forces. There is a strong imperative for Christians to address the injustice that is so wounding to Christ and so destructive of his creation. Jesus sets our agenda for us at the beginning of his own ministry in this way:

> The Spirit of the Lord is upon me, because he has anointed me to bring good news to the poor. He has sent me to proclaim release to the captives and recovery of sight to the blind, to let the oppressed go free, to proclaim the year of the Lord's favour.
>
> Luke 4:18-19

But the love of God, and our thirst for his justice, compels us to move beyond sentiment to strategy. That strategy needs to meet not only the requirements of the spirit but also the world's material needs. The fate of those who claim to worship and obey God yet neglect to implement such a practical strategy is graphically described by Amos in the quotation above.

There is a real need for a strategy, because there is real cause for anger. Anger, at the appalling housing conditions in which so many of our people have to live. Anger, at the number of men and women who have not had a job for a year or more and who are trapped in poverty and state dependency. Anger, at the plight of countless old age pensioners who fought in the War and worked hard for forty years or more and who still have to scrimp and save just to survive. Anger, too, at our heartless immigration laws and obstacles placed in the way of those people trying to flee here from persecution and oppression abroad [that's enough anger, Ed., as *Private Eye* would put it].

What then of hope? Hope springs from the certain knowledge of the power of good eventually to triumph over evil. There is ample evidence, if only we open our eyes to see it, of the capacity of the Holy Spirit, this thing that pours the love of God into our hearts and generates hope within us, to change and to transform not only ourselves and our relationships, but also the institutions of which we are a part.

We are required, however, to provide for the Holy Spirit a channel for his redemptive work, namely our own words and deeds in this world. The cross, an instrument of torture, degradation and death was transformed by the power of God into a symbol and instrument of liberation and life. Our own imperfect hearts, minds and talents must similarly be transformed into instruments capable of working compassion, love and justice in the world.

And the focus of this Christlike activity must be the local churches where we meet and worship. It is in and through the body of Christ in the local community that we can and must begin to make real, in our communal life and in the lives of our neighbours, what we believe about God and what we preach about the way things could be. Only then will people know that we share their anger and hurt at what pertains now, and only then will we be able to give people hope to work towards what could be in the future.

Hope is with Me

Mary Wilson

When in the night remorse returns to haunt me
And beat incessant drums inside my head,
And grief wells up for sympathy not given,
And lack of patient love for those now dead –

Then, in the darkness as I lie unsleeping,
Lost in the depths of three-o'clock despair,
The age-old cry comes to my mind unbidden
'Show me, O God, show me that you are there!'

But now a greyness creeps behind the curtain,
The birds awaken while it still is night
Blackbird and thrush, linnet and finch and starling,
Singing and carolling to greet the light.

High as the highest bell within the belfry,
In crystalline cascades of brilliant notes,
The chorus of the dawn, perfect in beauty
Rises in rapture from the beating throats.

And as the chilly air blows through the window,
The sun leaps upward in a yellow glow;
The last clear trembling voice falls into silence,
And am I answered now? I do not know.

I only know that as the daylight strengthens
The black dreams of the night are borne away;
I draw the curtain back to see the garden,
And hope is with me to begin the day.

I leant upon a coppice gate
    When Frost was spectre gray,
And winter's dregs made desolate
    The weakening eye of day.
The tangled bine stems scored the sky
    Like strings from broken lyres,
And all mankind that haunted nigh
    Had sought their household fires.

The land's sharp features seemed to be
    The Century's corpse outleant;
His crypt the cloudy canopy,
    The wind his death lament.
The ancient pulse of germ and birth
    Was shrunken hard and dry,
And every spirit upon earth
    Seemed fervourless as I.

At once a voice burst forth among
    The bleak twigs overhead
In full hearted evensong
    Of joy unlimited;
An aged thrush, frail, gaunt and small,
    In blast-beruffled plume,
Had chosen thus to fling his soul
    Upon the growing gloom.

So little cause for carollings
    Of such ecstatic sound
Was written on terrestial things
    Afar or nigh around,
That I could think there trembled through
    His happy good night air
Some blessed hope, whereof he knew
    And I was unaware.

Thomas Hardy, The Darkling Thrush

A conversation between a sensitive woman and a highly respected Christian monk:

'I've been believing all my life, but what if I die and there is nothing at all, and all that will happen is that 'burdock will be growing on my grave'. How am I to get back my faith? Mind you, I believed only when I was a little girl, mechanically, without thinking. But how am I to prove it? How is one to be convinced?'

'It's something one cannot prove. One can be convinced of it, though.'

'How? In what way?'

'By the experience of active love. Strive to love your neighbours actively and indefatigably. And the nearer you come to achieving this love, the more convinced you will become of the existence of God and the immortality of your soul.'

Feodor Dostoyevsky, *The Brothers Karamazov*

For him the problem was this, 'If I do not accept the answers Christianity gives to the questions of my life, what answers do I accept?' And in the whole arsenal of his convictions he failed to find not only any kind of answer but anything resembling an answer. He was in the position of a man seeking food in a toy shop or at a gunsmith's.

Leo Tolstoy, *Anna Karenina*

The demand for certainty is a sign of weakness, and if we persist in it induces paralysis. The successful man is he who, when he sees that no further certainty is available, promptly decides on the most probable side, as if he were completely sure it was right.

Mark Rutherford, *The Deliverance of Mark Rutherford*

In times of doubt and questionings, when our belief is perplexed by new learning, new teaching, new thought, when our faith is strained by creeds, by doctrines, by mysteries beyond our understanding, give us the faithfulness of learners and courage of believers in you; give us boldness to examine and faith to trust in all truth; patience and insight to master difficulties; stability to hold fast our tradition with enlightened interpretation, to admit all fresh truth made known to us, and in times of trouble to grasp new knowledge really and to combine it loyally and honestly with the old; insight to refrain from stubborn rejection of new revelations and from hasty assurance that we are wiser than our fathers.

George Ridding

My strength fails; I feel only weakness, irritation and depression. I am tempted to complain and to despair. What has become of the courage I was so proud of, and that gave me so much self-confidence? In addition to my pain, I have to bear the shame of my fretful feebleness. Lord, destroy my pride; leave it no resource. How happy I shall be if you can teach me by these terrible trials that I am nothing, and that I can do nothing, and that you are all!

Francois Fenelon

O soul, canst thou not understand
Thou art not left alone
As a dog to howl and moan
His master's absence? Thou art as a book
Left in a room that he forsook,
But returns to by and by,
A book of his dear choice,
That quiet waiteth for his Hand,
That quiet waiteth for his Eye,
That quiet waiteth for his Voice.

Michael Field, *Aridity*

When anxious, uneasy and bad thoughts come, I go to the sea, and the sea drowns them out with its great wide sounds, cleanses me with its noise and imposes a rhythm upon everything in me that is bewildered and confused.

Rainer Maria Rilke, *Letters*

In the evening at eight it [the storm] came, and rose higher and higher, after I thought it must have come to its strength . . . At last the long wished for morning came, but brought no abatement of the storm. There was so prodigious a sea that it quickly washed away our sheep and half our hogs, and drowned most of our fowl. The ship had been new caulked at Boston; how carefully, it now appeared; for being deeply laden, the sea streamed in at the side so plentifully, that it was as much as four men could do, by continual pumping, to keep her above water. I rose and lay down by turns, strove vehemently to pray, but in vain; persisted in striving, yet still without effect. I prayed for power to pray, for faith in Jesus Christ, continually repeating his name, till I felt the virtue of it at last, and knew that I abode under the shadow of the Almighty.

Charles Wesley, 28th October, 1736

Spirituality and the world of work – some reflections

Frances Young

Institutions

Relentless the turning wheels pursue the prophet of
　　God,
The spinning, crunching, crushing, relentless wheels of
　　fate,
The chariot wheels of power, the wheels of
　　establishment's will –
　　But the prophet outruns the wheels.

Relentless the turning wheels pursue the human race,
The spinning wheels of fate, winding the threads of
　　power,
Inexorable wheels of decisions made by machines,
Wheels within wheels within wheels within wheels –
　　the crushing wheels
That grind the dust and squeeze the juice of human
　　tears
To sap morale and break the back and bend the will –
　　But the prophet outruns the wheels.

Relentless the turning wheels, and all of us mere cogs
Caught on the wheel of birth, spun on the rim of the
　　world,
With structures reckoning our worth and systems
　　tapping the sap
And grinding human bones and stretching limbs on
　　the rack –
　　Now the prophet gets caught on the wheel

And his tortured body is mocked
And his head is crowned with thorns . . .
Then the turning stops,
  as the wheel breaks up,
    and a cross is formed
As a spoke is staked in the ground head high with
  arms outstretched.

Then all the wheels become winged wheels of fire
And the prophet rides the chariot higher and higher.

To appreciate this piece it is essential to remind
yourself of the story of Elijah (especially 1 Kings 18:46
and 2 Kings 2:11), as well as noting the allusions to the
Passion of Christ. It was written at a time when
institutional pressures seemed all against me and the
University Department of Theology for which I'm
responsible – in fact, when the pressures of 'middle
management' and bureaucracy seemed insurmount-
able. It expressed where I was in the world of work,
and I suspect where many people find themselves in
the huge institutional apparatuses now common,
where it is far from clear where power resides, or how
to get any change effected.

Yet the biblical images challenged the ideas of fate and
the 'wheel of birth' language which derive, of course,
from non-Christian sources, and generated an
unexpected hopeful conclusion, beyond any immediate
grounds. Strangely, since that 'rock-bottom' stage, the
tide has turned. The new systems that seemed so
threatening have in fact enabled the resurrection of the
Department and the rebuilding of the staff-team.

The Lecture

The expressed milk of the Word
Drops indiscriminately.
The ABC's of comprehensibility
Are caught in containers,
Refrigerated in files of notes,
Survival rations stored away
For brains to absorb
Whose grasp is premature.

Yet the light crumbles
And on some who've become as little children
Ideas are broken generously as bread of life.
Unleavened it cracks, brittle,
Brittle with sincerity and truth,
The sound of the still small voice
At the heart of the storm,
And the sharp simplicity
Of tradition lanced with the critical knife
Of complex questions.

Such is the discipline required
To digest the given-ness of solid food.
Who could be worthy
To place in the hand
The precious crumb of clarity?

Yet eucharist
Expresses the inexpressible,
Squeezing the grape
Into fountains of infinite reality,
Intoxicating the mind's eye with mystery,
Mediating the manna
Which rains indiscriminately
On wilderness ramblers.
Some are ready to receive
Singlemindedly,

Some are confident to consume
Wholeheartedly.
And then there is joy in heaven!

This piece is full of allusions, one to a poem by R. S. Thomas, some to the works of the great theologians and spiritual exegetes of Scripture from the early centuries of the Christian Church (the Greek 'Fathers' – my main research area), some to Scripture (1 Corinthians 2:1-2; Hebrews 5:12-14; Matthew 18:3; 1 Corinthians 5:8; 1 Kings 19:12 (AV); Hebrews 4:12; Exodus/John 6; Matthew 5:45; Luke 15:7).

Its composition was stimulated by a double frustration: (1) the experience of teaching students on what I sometimes call the 'sausage-machine' – they are there to get a degree, but they don't really know why, nor are they really engaged with a subject that is the burning passion of my life – they are just not on the same wavelength! What they want are neatly packaged bits of information, examination answers to be learned by rote; (2) the apparently fruitless struggle to take into the context of the University the deep things I had learned as a minister: how could I offer the bread of life to students of all kinds, some calling themselves Christians, others most definitely not?

Somehow the daring eucharistic image lifted me . . . The great thing about little children is that they are curious and relentless in their questioning, and that's what makes possible growth to maturity in understanding. Yet paradoxically, maturity is the ability to recognise the limitations of the human intellect, to discover that mastery is being mastered, and research is receptivity!

What is truth? Pilate's question rings down the centuries. Is it cynical or questing? hopeful or despairing? There is in any case immense irony – Pilate sits on the judgement seat and is judged.

Truth is now the most challenging and most threatened value. Petty deceits and cover-ups characterise day-to-day dealings, provoked by more and more explicit demands for accountability. Truth belongs to doing as well as being.

How will we stand when we discover that those characterised by 'singleness of heart' (i.e. integrity) bear the mark of the Lamb? The blessed are the pure in heart and those who hunger and thirst after righteousness – and that applies to filling in forms, paying dues, marking examinations, keeping records, responding to appeals panels, etc. etc.

We should ponder James 3:

Wisdom

The tongue
  small but damaging
a spark
  forest ravaging
a helm
  ship directing
a part
  whole deflecting
a beast
  untamed, brutal
a word
  unreined, cruel
a hurt
  inadvertent

a shameful
    defilement
a poison
    polluting
a spring
    salt-sweet sluicing
a jibe
    curse-inducing
a grace
    peace producing
a risk
    magnet fielding
the tongue
    power wielding.

* * *

Discernment is what we need.

Most of the time we are blind. The mood is one of
complaint, resistance to change, loss of morale; of
struggle and helplessness faced with increasing
student numbers, piles of marking, more and more
bureaucracy. Sometimes it seems the spirit has gone
out of it. That, of course, is the problem: those who
care about spiritual values, about literature and art,
language and music, culture and the past, feel
threatened by a world which only values transferable
skills and employability. Is that really all that higher
education is about?

We need renewal of vision, and a chance that some of
the young who grew up in Thatcher's years might even
catch on. The most important things are caught not
taught, but tell that to Teaching Quality Assessment!

Release

The tensions might create a tensile flame
that elongated tautens into sound,
a harp-string tuned to conduct the lightening-flash
   of angel's wings.

They might ring thought's bells – if flames didn't
   brand
or racks stretch high-strung to breaking-point
the broken life, silencing for good
   creative things.

They might – if the dark substitute image of sound
hadn't haunted the eyes, the shape of sound imploded,
snagged in self-silence, in passion for peace played
   on slackened strings.

   There's one who feels the pain
   as the self is tuned in the night
   to strain Air on a G string
   vibrating the candle light.

The teardrops might extinguish the guttering hope
that dimly eases updraughts into song
and so transfrees the gloom, tightening the calm
   that love brings.

They might dampen the heart's strings – if the fog of
   sound
hadn't lightened, muting confusion's loud pedal.
They might – if autumn's glow of grace didn't raise
   on eagle's wings.

   There's one who heals the hurt
   as the self is tuned to flight
   to soar stretched beyond tensions
   absorbing music's light.

The little cares that fretted me,
I lost them yesterday,
Among the fields above the sea,
Among the winds at play,
Among the lowing of the herds,
The rustling of the trees,
Among the singing of the birds,
The humming of the bees.

The foolish fears of what might pass
I cast them all away
Among the clover-scented grass
Among the new-mown hay,
Among the rustling of the corn
Where drowsy poppies nod,
Where ill thoughts die and good are born –
Out in the fields with God!

Author unknown

There are countless ways in which this [spiritual journey] may happen: sometimes under conditions which seem to the world like the very frustration of life, of progress, of growth. Thus boundless initiative is chained to a sick bed and transmuted into sacrifice; the lover of beauty is sent to serve in a slum, the lover of stillness is kept on the run all day, the sudden demand to leave all comes to the one who least expects it, and through and in these apparent frustrations the life of the spirit emerges and grows.

Evelyn Underhill, *The Spiritual Life*

I am twenty one today, the end and goal I have so often thought of. Up to this point I have been struggling, saying, 'When I am a man I shall do this, understand this, be great; now I am a boy and from a boy little is expected.' The sum of intellectual progress I hoped for has been obtained, but how much below my hopes. My character has developed, but in what puny proportions, below my meanest anticipations. I do not feel a man. This book is an evidence of the yearnings without power, and the brooding self-analysis without creation that afflict me. I am not a man.

J. Addington Symonds, *Diary*, 5th October, 1861

He pondered much on serious subjects and like all thoughtful and earnest men, his faith was somewhat overcast. He chanced just then to read the life of Mahomet. It awoke in his mind sceptical doubts. Perplexed and distressed, he listened, prayed and read, in agonising anxiety, to find out whether the New Testament or the Koran was the true revelation, whether Jesus or Mahomet was the true prophet. At last, the patient study of the Bible brought before him Hebrews 7:26, which dispelled his doubts for ever.

Elizabeth Davis, *Autobiography*
Ed. Jane Williams

I wonder if the sap is stirring yet,
If wintry birds are dreaming of a mate,
If frozen snowdrops feel as yet the sun
And crocus fires are kindling one by one;
    Sing, robin, sing;
I still am sore in doubt concerning Spring.

Christina Rossetti, The First Spring Day

If a man will begin with certainties he shall end in doubt; but if he will be content to begin with doubt, he shall end in certainties.

Francis Bacon, *The Advancement of Learning*

This is what I see and what troubles me. I look in every direction and all I see is darkness. Nature has nothing to offer me that does not give rise to doubt and anxiety. If I saw no sign of a Divinity I should decide on a negative solution; if I saw signs of a creator everywhere I should peacefully settle down in the faith. But seeing too much to deny and not enough to affirm, I am in a pitiful state, where I have wished a hundred times over, that if there is a God supporting nature, she should unequivocally proclaim him; and that if the signs of nature are deceptive, they should be completely erased; that nature should say all or nothing so that I could see what course I ought to follow . . . My whole heart strains to know what the true good is in order to pursue it; no price would be too high to pay for eternity.

Blaise Pascal, *Pensées*

I had utterly given up the whole problem of religion as insoluble. I believed in poetry, science, and democracy – and they were enough for me then; enough, at least, to leave a mighty hunger in my heart, I knew not for what.

Charles Kingsley

Where is the foolish person who would think it in his power to commit more sins than God could forgive? and who will dare to measure by the greatness of his crimes, the immensity of that infinite mercy which casts them all into the depths of the sea of oblivion, when we repent of them with love?

St Francis de Sales

After this our Lord showed me about prayer. The result of this revelation is that I now see that there are two conditions about prayer. One concerns rightness, the other our sure trust. Often enough our trust is not wholehearted, for we are not sure that God hears us. We think it is due to our unworthiness and because we feel absolutely nothing; we are often as barren and dry after our prayers as we were before. This awareness of our foolishness is the cause of our weakness. At least this has been my own experience.

Julian of Norwich

I have become more and more desirous to be religious, but seem to be further off than ever. Whenever I draw near, the negative side of the magnet works, and I am pushed back by an invisible power.

Henry Crabb Robinson, *Diary*, 31st December, 1823

One thing we owe to Our Lord is never to be afraid. To be afraid is doubly an injury to him. Firstly, it means that we forget him; we forget he is with us and is all powerful; secondly, it means that we are not conformed to his will; for since all that happens is willed or permitted by him, we ought to rejoice in all that happens to us and feel neither anxiety nor fear. Our Lord is at our side, with us, upholding us.

Charles de Foucauld, *Meditations of a Hermit*

Negative capability, that is when a man is capable of being in uncertainties, mysteries, doubts without any irritable reaching after fact and reason.

John Keats

Each of us seeks a treasure. It is elusive and difficult to achieve. It attracts us even when we aren't sure of its contents. The longing for it sustains us on rough and dangerous terrain. In the searching we already possess the sought-for. We journey all the days of our lives, with hope in our hearts, led by the Spirit. One day there dawns the realisation that we must give all we possess in exchange for the pearl of great price. In the end, the one 'who searches hearts' knows our spirit and our intention, and it is God's glory that is revealed in us.

Joan Puls, *Every Bush is Burning*

Doubt

Frank Collier

One of my saddest memories is of a teenage boy who, on being asked what gift he would appreciate above anything else, replied that he wished someone would make him a promise which they did not break. He had had a chequered childhood, moved from one foster home to another and from one school to another until he was quite unable to trust people around him. His human universe filled him with all pervading doubt.

So, happy are they who as children are able to put aside both doubts and fears because they know that there are those whom they can trust. It is a matter for concern that today children perforce must be discouraged from trusting strangers. One can only fear the ultimate effect on their capacity for trust and faith. He who cannot trust his fellows will find it hard to trust God.

More important still, however, is the inner universe of thought and feeling, of will and intention. Self-doubt which springs from our secret knowledge of ourselves is crippling. To know that we have a temper which runs out of control or that we lack the courage to be truthful when trouble looms, makes us very insecure under pressure. Simply to be aware that we are not quite the persons that the world thinks we are can prevent us from responding readily to friendship. Add a little shyness and there is the making of a very lonely person.

As a child I could be quite sure that my parents' word would be kept and I could sleep quite securely. But I also inherited a questioning disposition from my father, which meant that side by side with religious faith there travelled a curiosity which was quite insatiable. Education transformed that curiosity into a burgeoning scepticism.

I was encouraged to question the conclusions of the scholars whose works I read. It was imperative that I brought a savagely critical eye to documents I studied. Nothing must be accepted without adequate proof. My success or failure as a student depended on that developed ability to doubt.

Thus firmly established, doubt is not easily confined to scholastic matters. But for a young person from a very religious background it can entail horrible feelings of guilt. To question the Bible, to wonder secretly whether the story of the Resurrection was not fabricated by enthusiasts and to have doubts about the evidence of Christ's life story seemed almost blasphemous.

Honesty, however, won the day, and rightly so. Faith cannot be defended by dishonest means. If my mind could not be brought to accept what politicians said or preachers proclaimed, then so much the worse for political and religious dogmas. My mind must be respected. I could not possess either political convictions or religious faith until my reason was satisfied.

I took comfort in the exhortations of some seventeenth century Christians in refusing to quell doubt in the name of faith. For instance, Benjamin Whichcote said:

To go against Reason, is to go against God; it is the selfsame thing, to do that which the Reason of the case doth require; . . . Reason is the Divine Governor of Man's Life; it is the very Voice of God.

In face of doubt such authority could be very encouraging.

At the outset we are constrained to doubt what cannot be proved. The student's rightful deference to evidence is transferred to the realm of faith. But a combination of Whichcote and William Temple came to the rescue. Whichcote had drawn a distinction;

Reason discovers what is Natural; and Reason receives what is Supernatural.

Archbishop Temple drew a subtler distinction. Speaking at a university mission he told the story of a woman student who had strenuously asserted that she would never believe anything which could not be proved. Ascertaining that she was reading English he asked which she considered to be the greatest poem in the English language. Unhesitatingly she chose Milton's sonnet 'On His Blindness'. He then asked if she knew the hymn 'Hark! Hark, my soul! Angelic songs are swelling'. She nodded and was then asked for her judgement on the relative quality of the poem and the hymn as poetry.

As strenuously as she had asserted her religious doubts she asserted her strong belief in the value of Milton's poem. Her confidence only ebbed and finally disappeared when the Archbishop asked her to prove that her belief was true. She discovered that over a great area of human experience what we believe and hold dear is quite beyond proof. The eye of the poet and the artist is quite different from that of the physicist, and yet no one would deny that the insight of Milton or Rembrandt has its own place in the treasury of human experience.

That hurdle cleared it is possible to see doubt as a blessing rather than a curse. Faith can be strengthened by doing battle with insistent questionings whether regarding the Bible, Christian doctrines, or moral dilemmas. And when experience of great anxiety, sorrow or penitence has for a time shadowed faith, recovery has often made the faith all the stronger.

That does not mean that there are not times when quiescent, lingering doubt cannot be activated and prove deeply disconcerting and distressing. Tennyson was shaken by the thought of 'nature red in tooth and claw'. J. S. Mill felt till the very end of his life that the savagery of nature meant that there could not possibly be a God who was both all powerful and all loving. If God was all powerful he must in deference to his own love halt the carnage. If he did not do so, then either the power or the love were absent. A diet of contemporary nature films intensifies the questioning.

Human suffering too can awaken darkening doubts. The spectacle of one human life which seems to have been exposed to almost unbroken pain and loss cannot surely leave the Christian with an undisturbed peace of mind. The death of an only child or the long drawn out suffering of a fine Christian seem increasingly to try our faith the more we are moved to compassion.

Pious platitudes avail little, and occasionally give the impression of callous indifference to suffering. Perhaps there is only one assurance adequate for us. We remember that Christ himself passed through the darkest time of doubt and desolation. With no-one he could entirely trust even among his closest friends, with his faith mocked and the God he served somehow veiled in darkness, he knew that emptiness which attends the loss of faith, if only for a very short time. And at length he carried that doubt and emptiness into the heart of God. So what we experience God has experienced too. We need not be ashamed but rather know that he is with us in the darkness of doubt.

Contributors

Kriss Akabusi, MBE is well known for his achievements in athletics. He began his international career in 1983, as a member of the British 4 x 400 metre relay squad, and in 1991 was part of the team which won gold medals in the World Championships 4 x 400 metre relay in Tokyo. His greatest individual triumph was a gold medal in the 1990 European Championships 400 metre hurdles.

Marilyn Baker was born in Birmingham. She attended a school for the blind in Chorleywood and then went on to the Royal School of Music, where she studied oboe and piano. Marilyn became a Christian as a teenager and began writing Christian songs while still at college. She now sings at many concerts and Christian events.

Alan Beith, MP is Deputy Leader and Home Affairs spokesman of the Liberal Democrats, and has been Liberal Democrat MP for Berwick upon Tweed since 1973. He is a member of the House of Commons Commission, the Intelligence and Security Committee and the Historic Chapels Trust. He is a member of the Methodist Church and a local preacher.

Ann Bird is Pastoral Care Secretary for the Methodist Church's Division of Ministries which involves resourcing pastoral carers and raising awareness about many pastoral concerns. Her work is focused particularly on spirituality and pastoral care, crisis care, disability and care of the ordained ministry. She also writes on pastoral care subjects.

Paul Boateng, MP was the first person of African descent to be elected to the British Parliament, when he became MP for Brent South in 1987. He served on the Shadow Treasury team under John Smith until 1992 when he was appointed Labour's Legal Affairs Spokesman. He is a Methodist local preacher and a former Vice-Moderator of the World Council of Churches' Programme to Combat Racism.

Dr Sheila Cassidy is the Medical Director of St Luke's Hospice in Plymouth. As a young doctor she went to work in Chile where she became caught up in the oppressive regime which resulted in her arrest, imprisonment, torture and finally her expulsion from the country. She is now a preacher and broadcaster and the author of several books, including *Good Friday People* (Darton, Longman and Todd) and *Light from the Dark Valley: Reflections on Suffering and the Care of the Dying* (Darton, Longman and Todd).

Rev Dr Emilio Castro was born in Uruguay. He is an ordained pastor in the Evangelical Methodist Church in Uruguay, and from 1965-73 he was Co-ordinator of the Commission for Evangelical Unity in Latin America (UNELAM). He then became Director of the World Council of Churches' Commission on World Mission and Evangelism, which he held until the end of 1983. In 1985 Emilio Castro became the WCC's fourth General Secretary.

Lord Coggan was Principal of the London College of Divinity, and in 1956 was appointed Bishop of Bradford. He became Archbishop of York in 1961, and from 1974-1980 he was Archbishop of Canterbury. He is the author of several books including *God of Hope* (Fount), *Servant Son: Jesus Then and Now* (Triangle) and *Voice from the Cross: Seven words of Jesus* (Triangle).

Frank Collier has spent much of his professional life in teaching Religious Education, and has been an active Methodist local preacher for over fifty-three years. He has written a number of study series for his local house groups at Rhos-on-Sea Methodist Church; these include *The Parables of Jesus, The Lord's Prayer* and *The Beatitudes* (Foundery Press).

Rev Dr Donald English is a Minister in the Methodist Church who has served as a Circuit Minister, a theological teacher and General Secretary of the Methodist Church's Home Mission Division. He is Chairman of the World Methodist Council. His particular concern is how Christian believing makes sense of life.

Rev Dr M. Stanley Mogoba is the Presiding Bishop of the Methodist Church of Southern Africa, one of the country's largest multi-racial churches. Rooted in Methodism, he spent almost four years in Robben Island prison for so-called political offences against the State. Recently appointed co-Chairman with Archbishop Desmond Tutu for the Peace Accord, Dr Mogoba has been in the forefront of the Church's fight against apartheid.

Maureen Newcombe is a Methodist local preacher and is on the General Committee of the Methodist Local Preachers' Mutual Aid association. She is also a CRUSE bereavement counsellor.

Canon Michael Saward has had a varied ministry: two curacies, Secretary of Liverpool Council of Churches, Anglican Radio and Television Officer and Vicar of two West London parishes. He is a Church Commissioner and member of the General Synod and also works as an author, preacher and broadcaster. He has been Treasurer of St Paul's Cathedral since 1991.

Jean Vanier was born in Canada. In 1964 he founded l'Arche, in Trosly-Breuil, northern France, a community with men and women who have learning disabilities, many coming from psychiatric centres. From this original community one hundred and five others have been founded throughout the world, including seven in the United Kingdom. Jean Vanier now divides his life between visiting and encouraging the various communities, writing and lecturing. His books include *Community and Growth* (Darton, Longman and Todd) and *Jesus, the Gift of Love* (Hodder and Stoughton).

Rosemary Wakelin is a Methodist Minister in the Norwich Circuit. She trained as a missionary at Selly Oak College and with her husband Dr Paul Wakelin served in Sierra Leone and Kenya. She taught for thirty years and has also broadcast on radio and television for twenty-five years.

Pauline Warner has been a Methodist Minister for twelve years and is currently serving in the Coventry Circuit. She has made a special study of Mary, the mother of Jesus, and a second area of study is women's ministry in the Church. She is the author of *For Your Maker is Your Husband* (Epworth Press).

Rev William Watty, a native of Dominica, has served in the British Virgin Islands and the South and North Trinidad Circuits of the Methodist Church in the Caribbean and the Americas (MCCA), and was President of the United Theological College of the West Indies, Jamaica. He was Chairman of the South Caribbean District from 1985-1990 before becoming President of the Conference.

Rev Stanley J. West is presently the General Secretary of the Methodist Church of New Zealand, Te Haahi Weteriana o Aotearoa, a position he has held for eight years. He has also served in a number of parishes and as Synod Secretary and District Superintendent. As part of his ministry he has been accredited as both a Marriage Counsellor and Supervisor.

Mary Wilson, the wife of Lord Wilson of Rievaulx, was born at Diss, the daughter of a Congregational Minister. She was educated at Milton Mount College (now Wentworth Milton Mount) a school for Ministers' daughters. She began to write poetry at the age of six and has published three volumes of verse.

Rev Professor Frances Young studied Classics in London and Theology in Cambridge and Chicago. She has lectured in Theology at the University of Birmingham since 1971, and in 1986 she became Edward Cadbury Professor and Head of the Department of Theology. She was ordained as a Methodist Minister in 1984.

Acknowledgements

The publishers would like to express their gratitude to Mr Frank Collier for his invaluable help in compiling this book.

Methodist Publishing House gratefully acknowledge permission to include copyright items. Every effort has been made to trace copyright owners, but where we have been unsuccessful we would welcome information which would enable us to make appropriate acknowledgement in any reprint.

'More than Champions' by Kriss Akabusi is taken from *More than Champions* by Stuart Weir, published by HarperCollins Publishers.

'Reconciliation' by Emilio Castro is taken from *A Passion for Unity:* Essays on ecumenical hope and challenges by Emilio Castro © 1992, WCC Publications, World Council of Churches, P.O. Box 2100, 1211 Geneva 2, Switzerland. Used with permission.

'Return to Chile' by Sheila Cassidy originally appeared in *The Tablet* and is reproduced by kind permission of the Editor. (The Tablet, 1 King Street Cloisters, Clifton Walk, London W6 0QZ.)

A. S. J. Tessimond, 'Daydream', *The Collected Poems of A. S. J. Tessimond, with translations from Jacques Prévert*, edited by Hubert Nicholson (Whiteknights Press, 1985).

Ulrich Simon, *A Theology of Auschwitz* (originally published by Victor Gollancz) quoted in *Each in his Prison* by Elizabeth Bassett (SPCK).

'Let Joy Break Out', reproduced from *Liturgy of Life* compiled by Donald Hilton with the permission of the National Christian Education Council.

Kilvert's Diary, The Estate of Francis Kilvert, Jonathan Cape.

Robert Brizee, *Where in the World is God?* Copyright © by The Upper Room. Used by permission of the publisher.

Christopher Smart, 'A Song to David' from *Praise Above All* by A. M. Allchin, University of Wales Press.

Michel Quoist, *With Open Heart*, Gill and MacMillan Publishers.

Gordon MacDonald, *Restoring your Spiritual Passion*, Highland Books.

Henri Nouwen, *Life Signs*, HarperCollins Publishers.

Paul Tillich, *The New Being*, SCM Press 1956.

Elizabeth Davis, *Autobiography*, Ed. Jane Williams, Honno Cardiff.

Charles de Foucauld, *Meditations of a Hermit*, Burns & Oates.

Joan Puls, OSF, *Every Bush is Burning: A Spirituality for our Times* © 1985 WCC Publications, World Council of Churches, Geneva, Switzerland.

Sydney Carter, 'My Believing Bones,' from *The Two Way Clock*. Reproduced by permission of Stainer & Bell Ltd.

Elizabeth Yates, *Up the Golden Stair*, Copyright © 1990. Used by permission of The Upper Room.

James A. Harnish, *Jesus makes the Difference!* Copyright © 1987 by The Upper Room. Used by permission of the publisher.

Havelock Ellis, *Essays*, by permission of Professor Francois Lafitte.

Rufus M. Jones, *The Double Search*, reprinted with permission of Friends United Press of Richmond, Indiana, copyright 1975.